D1563945

people walk on their heads

Moses Weinberger's
Jews and Judaism in New York

TRANSLATED FROM THE HEBREW AND EDITED BY

JONATHAN D. SARNA

Holmes and Meier Publishers, Inc.

New York • London

F
128.9
.J5
W413
1982

First published in the United States of America 1982 by
Holmes & Meier Publishers, Inc.
30 Irving Place, New York, N.Y. 10003

Great Britain:
Holmes & Meier Publishers, Ltd.
131 Trafalgar Road
Greenwich, London SE10 9TX

Library of Congress Cataloging in Publication Data

Weinberger, Moses, b. 1865.
  People walk on their heads.

    Translation of: ha-Yehudim veha-Yahadut be-Nuyork.
    Includes index.
    1. Jews—New York (N.Y.)   2. Judaism—New York
(N.Y.)   3. New York (N.Y.)—Ethnic relations.   I. Sarna,
Jonathan D.   II. Title.
F128.9.J5W413   1982   974.7'1004924   81-6907
ISBN 0-8419-0707-2   AACR2
        0-8419-0731-5 pbk.

Printed in the United States of America

Design by Marsha Picker

To David, Rachel, and Ariel

Contents

Editor's Foreword

Moses Weinberger's *Jews and Judaism in New York* (1887) might have been an immigrant classic. Its subject is the greatest Jewish city in the world. Its style is lively, often bitingly satiric. Its portrayal is brilliant, graphic, and strikingly original. Yet *Jews and Judaism in New York* lies unnoticed and unread. The remarkable history of East European Jewish immigration, Irving Howe's *World of Our Fathers*, ignores the book; it knows Weinberger only through another source. Moses Rischin's pathbreaking *The Promised City: New York's Jews 1870–1914* relegates Weinberger to a lonely footnote.

The neglect is perhaps understandable. Few copies of the volume exist, probably no more than twenty-five. Worse still, the volume appeared in Hebrew. Many who may have wanted to read the book found it beyond their linguistic capabilities. The book has therefore remained the exclusive property of the specially trained. Nobody has ever done the volume full justice.

Moses Weinberger deserved better. His book, which I analyze at greater length in the Introduction, is the best single source for Orthodox Jewish life among early East European immigrants to New York. Not only does it deal with subjects usually neglected—ritual functionaries, beggars, Hebrew teachers, and the like—but it presents a strikingly different perspective on immigration as a whole. Unlike gushing Mary Antin, who viewed America (*The Promised Land*) through rose-colored glasses, and unlike socialist entrepreneur Abraham Cahan, whose heroes succeeded only insofar as they stopped being "green" and started moving forward, Weinberger extols conservative rebels: Jews who resist

1

Americanization, remaining fully loyal to their tradition. Progress to Weinberger means the founding of a yeshiva for Talmud study, the strengthening of ritual observance, and the establishment of a powerful, cohesive rabbinic leadership.

Jews and Judaism in New York forms part of a larger literature, one that remains largely unexplored by scholars. This is the literature of immigrant protest penned by pious newcomers who found America an amoral, materialistic land, "a world turned upside-down." Socialism, reform, and revolution held no appeal to these "defenders of the faith"; they aimed to return America to normalcy via time-tested means. Scorning America as found, they sketched out an America as it could be if religious leaders were restored to their rightful place. They dared to speak out for "tradition," even as the cry of "progress" swirled around them.

In translating *Jews and Judaism in New York*, I have endeavored to meet obligations due both my text and my readers. I lay no claim to complete success; indeed, I hope that the original may soon be made available to all who can understand it. While I agree with Karl Popper that "every good translation must be at the same time close *and* free," I know from experience that the two aims are irreconcilable. Unfortunately the tension between them is no easier to resolve for having been stated.

Moses Weinberger was a skilled if careless author, writing in a language—Hebrew—that was not his native tongue. His Hebrew typifies learned Hebrew writing of the day: peppered with biblical and rabbinic phrases, and punctuated with flowery conceits. At times his sentences extend for a full paragraph; some paragraphs continue on for pages. Footnotes are bulky and burdensome; chapter divisions, with one exception, do not exist. As editor I have decided to spare the reader many of these inconveniences. I have introduced chapters and paragraphs, and divided long sentences. I have incorporated most footnotes into the text (several footnotes have been relegated to a new section called "Author's Notes") and I have taken the liberty of silently correcting obvious typographical errors. Where the Hebrew is particularly flowery and redundant, I have felt free to employ a simplified idiom. But I have not abbreviated the basic text at all. The only exceptions to this rule may be found in the Publisher's Preface and the Author's Appendix, where I have dropped lengthy literary conceits—irrelevant paraphrases from rabbinic literature. Otherwise I have been careful to place all material not originally found in the Weinberger text either in square brackets or in numbered notes. Most background information may be found in the Introduction.

Werner Weinberg's *How Do You Spell Chanukah? A General Purpose Romanization of Hebrew for Speakers of English* (Cincinnati, 1976) has spared me considerable grief in the matter of transliteration. I have Romanized according to a modified Ashkenazic system, since that is closer to the Hebrew spoken by Weinberger himself. In the case of proper nouns, I have employed standard English equivalents when available. Important foreign terms may be found defined in the Glossary.

I am grateful to the staffs of the American Jewish Archives, Klau Library (Cincinnati), Sterling Memorial Library, Widener Library, Hebrew College Library, and the American Jewish Historical Society for their unfailing courtesy to me during the course of my research. Hebrew Union College–Jewish Institute of Religion generously extended aid to me in the form of Miriam November's expert typing. Its president, Dr. Alfred Gottschalk, has shown unstinting interest in my work, and indeed in all facets of the American Jewish experience. Mr. Zachary Baker of Yivo, Professor Jeffrey Gurock of Yeshiva University, my father, Professor Nahum M. Sarna of Brandeis University, and Dr. Alexander Guttmann of Hebrew Union College–Jewish Institute of Religion, all rendered to me invaluable assistance with specific questions. Rabbi Lance Sussman of Hebrew Union College–Jewish Institute of Religion, Professor William Toll of the American Jewish Archives, Professor Jerome Mushkat of the University of Akron, and Professor Benny Kraut of the University of Cincinnati made exceedingly helpful comments on earlier drafts of my introduction. Dr. Abraham J. Peck, associate director of the American Jewish Archives, has been a consistently helpful and warm friend. My debt to Professor Jacob Rader Marcus—mentor, colleague, and friend—is incalculable. I should also like to recognize Dr. Eisig Silberschlag in whose classroom I first learned about translations, their problems, and much, much more.

I have dedicated this volume in love and gratitude to my brother, sister-in-law, and nephew. New York is their favorite city. They represent modern day "Jews and Judaism in New York" at its best—even if they do now live in New Jersey.

J. D. S.

Editor's Introduction

In 1880, Moses Weinberger (1854–1940) arrived in New York City from Kniesen, Zips (Szepes), Hungary.[1] He was twenty-six years old, staunchly Orthodox, and freshly trained in the rabbinate. He left Hungary, seemingly against his will, for reasons unknown. Whatever those reasons may have been, New York was the wrong place for him. True, the city then already had an Orthodox Jewish population estimated to number 10,000 people.[2] It housed an impressive Hungarian congregation, Ohab Zedek, founded in 1872/3, as well as several other Orthodox synagogues, most notably Beth Hamedrash Hagodc! '1852, reorganized 1859), Beth Hamedrash Livne Yisroel Yelide Polen (1853, later the Kalvarier Shul) and Khal Adas Jeshurun (1856). But these synagogues lived in relative poverty; most lacked the money to support a full-time rabbi.[3] And if any did want a rabbi, they had little trouble luring one with distinguished European credentials, reports of ritual laxity in America notwithstanding. When, for example, Bet Hamidrash Hagodol Ubnai Jacob, the leading Orthodox congregation in Chicago, sought a rabbi—in the very year Weinberger arrived in New York—they were able to coax the renowned Abraham Jacob Gerson Lesser (1834–1925) from Ludwinow, Suwalki. They did not need to look for a young upstart.[4]

So Moses Weinberger found no rabbinical post. In spite of his impressive scholarly credentials—he was at various times a student of such Hungarian luminaries as Rabbis Meier Perles, Samuel Ehrenfeld, Eleazar Loew, and Moses Sofer (d. 1917, not to be confused with his namesake known as the Chasam Sofer)[5]—circumstances forced him to try his hand at various sorts of business. He kept up his studies in his spare time, ministered to those of his countrymen who approached him, became president of a newly formed Hungarian congregation, engaged in learned correspondence with European rabbis, and wrote occasional pieces in Jewish periodicals. But he was far from happy with his lot. His letter to a friend (1887), reprinted in the Appendix to this volume, exudes nostalgia for the world that he and his family had lost forever.[6]

Jews and Judaism in New York, published in Hebrew in 1887, represents Weinberger's attempt to draw together what seven years' experience had taught him about the land he had now to call his own. The book originally appeared as a pamphlet, 124 pages long, and the proceeds from its sale were dedicated to the Machzike Talmud Thora Institute, a Hebrew Free School devoted to "perpetuation of the Jewish religion . . . according to the old Orthodox ritual." Like Weinberger, leaders of the Machzike Talmud Thora believed in revitalizing time-tested religious ways. They taught traditional subjects in the same manner and the same language—Yiddish—as had been done for centuries. The relationship between the school and the book was a natural one.[7]

Had *Jews and Judaism in New York* aimed at a mass audience, it might have been written in Yiddish, the immigrant vernacular. But Moses Weinberger sought a more limited readership: learned, ritually observant Jews. He therefore wrote in Hebrew. Rabbis normally used the holy tongue to convey their thoughts; it lent prestige to their words and guaranteed that rabbis and scholars all over the world, even in non-Yiddish-speaking lands, could understand them. Besides, Weinberger was a lover of Zion, a supporter if not indeed a member of proto-Zionist societies.[8] In this he was indirectly influenced, as were many Hungarian rabbis, by the Chasam (Moses) Sofer (1762–1839), the great leader of Hungarian Orthodoxy. The Chasam Sofer wrote in Hebrew; his students wrote in Hebrew. For Weinberger to have employed any other language would have been unthinkable.

Moses Weinberger's intended audience divided naturally into two groups: those considering emigration to America and those who had already immigrated. The first group—young East European scholars, aspiring rabbis like himself—received a blunt message: "Stay home." As far as Weinberger was concerned, New York City was America in micro-cosm. What he learned about the one he applied to the other. In addressing his peer group abroad, he generalized accordingly:

> Nothing will be left for you to do save dressing in black, wrapping yourself in shrouds, and rolling from darkness to

abyss: from factory to sweatshop to itinerant peddling. For such great successes you don't need America! You don't need to endanger your life by crossing great stretches of water! There, in your homeland and your own little city, you can do just as well if you only work diligently and put all fears of shame behind you.

Weinberger knew that many Jewish immigrants of his day, particularly romantic intellectuals and idealistic scholars, became quickly disenchanted with Columbus's land and returned to Europe. He tried to spare them all that expense and hardship by telling them what to expect in advance.[9]

Weinberger's second audience, those already in America, hardly needed to be told that a yawning gap existed between America as dreamed about and America as found. For them *Jews and Judaism in New York* functioned as a kind of sociological analysis. It brought facts into focus, identified problems, and proposed solutions. Weinberger treated all major areas of Jewish life in New York: synagogues, kosher food, education, work, culture, ritual functionaries, charity, and more. He generalized broadly in each case, but often backed up his words with "case studies," anecdotes drawn from personal experience. Of course, he made no pretense to scientific objectivity. Instead, as the Publisher's Preface promised, he endeavored "to uncover . . . the method by which the great wall of religion against which all Israel rests can be fortified."

Rather than summarizing *Jews and Judaism in New York*, I aim in what follows to employ its insights to understand better how traditional immigrant Judaism was transformed on American soil. The passage of time permits a broader perspective on the data Weinberger supplied. We can now appreciate the significance of changes he could merely chronicle. Perhaps the complex dynamic relationship among immigration, religion, and forces of acculturation will never be completely unraveled. With Weinberger's works before us, analysis can at least begin.[10]

Jews and Judaism in New York examines the Jewish community under three lenses. It employs the widest lens to analyze America's impact on immigrant Judaism. It shows how democracy, church-state separation, and the spirit of capitalism all affected the relationship of Jews to their religion. A narrower focus reveals complex dealings between different sectors of the New York Jewish community. Jews lived uptown and downtown; identified as Orthodox, Conservative, and Reform; and divided into radical and nonradical camps. The immigrant Orthodox felt kindred to all these groups, whether they agreed with them or not. In its narrowest focus, the book concentrates on New York's East Side Orthodox community. Here Weinberger truly showed his mastery. No better portrayal exists.

The wide-angle lens of *Jews and Judaism in New York* focuses almost at once on American democracy: the impact on immigrant Jews of egalitarian ideals so much at variance with the deferential system they knew in Europe. Weinberger found many communal leaders without learning, piety, or wealth; they were, in his phrase, "tanners"—boorish hand laborers who would in their native lands receive scant attention. According to the Talmud (Kidushin 82b), "The world cannot exist without a perfumer and without a tanner; happy is the man whose craft is perfuming and woe to the man who is a tanner by trade." Yet in America Weinberger saw the "tanners," or their ilk, become everyone's equal. They outvoted the learned, made policy on their own, and aspired to high synagogue office.[11] In America, Weinberger observed, elections took place frequently, decisions were subject to group discussion, and meetings occurred almost daily. Politics replaced study as the central synagogue activity.

Weinberger blamed immigrants' infatuation with democracy on American society's belief that "equal hats make men equal." Democracy, he implied, could not coexist with traditional Jewish learning habits, for it scorned time-honored scholarly prerogatives. Viewed more broadly, however, the shift from study hall to meeting hall represents one facet of a larger transformation from East European Judaism to American Judaism. Formerly, particularly where the Enlightenment had not taken hold, Jews tended to look inward; they modeled themselves after the best of their own nation. They now looked outward and consciously adopted the values of their neighbors. Study as an end in itself had traditionally been a form of cultural rebellion; it set Jews apart from surrounding peoples and helped them feel superior, even when to all outward appearances their position seemed inferior in the extreme. "We arise early and they arise early: we for Torah and they for nonsense. . . . We run and they run; we to the world to come and they to hell." The dictum, part of the *siyum* ceremony celebrating the completed study of a talmudic tractate, spelled out the core value system that maintained Jewish morale in the midst of persecution. No matter who won in this world, Jews, on account of their constant study, felt sure they would win in the end.

America challenged this value system. Immigrant Jews found that, in the New World, power—the capacity to shape people and events—was a core value, education being important only insofar as it furthered this end. The politicizing of synagogue and group life was thus a bow to modernity. It symbolized Jews' acceptance of secular values, and anticipated—as well as reflected—their rapid entry into secular society. Jews continued to value study—indeed, Weinberger described how a lodge meeting he attended began with words of Torah—but learning ceased to be a value in and of itself. It, rather, became a handmaiden of power, offering the stamp of Jewish legitimacy to those who rose to the top through other means. The synthesis of leadership and learning became, in Jewish eyes, the synthesis of America and Jew. Those who brought about this fusion could expect to win Jewish support both in the religious world and in the secular one.

If American democracy affected all aspects of immigrant Judaism, reaching down even into its core values, the impact of church-state separation was no less pervasive:

> In all other lands a man is required by the government to belong to the *kehilah* [community] of the area where he lives, and like it or not it levies taxes upon him. In America, any man may cut himself off from his community, taking no part in it whatsoever.

Here as elsewhere Weinberger exaggerated America's uniqueness. By 1887 a large percentage of European Jewry no longer lay under *kehilah* rule either. The impact of government nonintervention, however, was bound to make a profound impression on a Hungarian Jew. In Hungary Jewish authority drew much of its legitimacy and power directly from the government. Rabbis convinced the authorities to back up their religious regulations with the force of law, arguing that if they didn't, the Jewish community might crumble and disappear altogether. The contrast with America, where in most states even marriages did not require religious sanction, could not have been greater. The state would offer Judaism no support at all. Weinberger understood this, and warned Jewish leaders that, in the New World, customary tactics—rabbinical congresses and appeals to secular powers—would prove ineffective. But it took considerably longer for immigrant rabbis to discover what would prove effective. Orthodoxy had to learn what all religious groups in America must inevitably learn: in a voluntary state, religion can operate only by persuasion.

Weinberger failed to appreciate the power of persuasion. He was struck by the impact of capitalism on American Jews, immigrants and natives alike. As he saw it, money alone had become their god: "That's the principle. That's the goal. That's honor, strength, and the only reliably acceptable testimony. For most people in this city and nation, that is the single basis upon which all is evaluated." The observation, of course, was not original. No American characteristic received more attention or criticism. Weinberger showed originality only when he went beyond this ritualistic animadversion to demonstrate how Orthodoxy could harness this entrepreneurial spirit for its own benefit. He realized, as many of his colleagues did not, that the religion business—"*mitzvah* merchants"—ultimately served to strengthen Jewish practice. As the business-minded made ritual objects cheaper and more accessible, more people used them. The easier Judaism was to observe, the more people observed it. In a sense, the "*mitzvah* merchant" was a Jewish revivalist in disguise.[12]

Weinberger's ability to praise those who profited from religion accords with his oft-stated opinion that America was "a world turned upside-down."

> ... in America nothing is impossible. Just as America could invent the telephone, and transform many another wonder into a commonplace, so it can surely change the spirit of man by making the fools wiser, and the wise more foolish.

The pronouncement is sarcastic, but reflects a common myth. Immigrants and foreign visitors expected to find American values alien, at times diametrically opposed to what they had known before. They believed that democracy, church-state separation, the entrepreneurial spirit, and other peculiarly American phenomena combined to make "anything possible." In the New World nothing would surprise them.

Weinberger both perpetuated this myth and pointed out that it was not quite true. Many changes had taken place, and others could be expected. Yet Weinberger knew that many a seeming transformation was more apparent than real. The fools only *appeared* to grow wiser in America; in fact they were just as foolish as ever. Some things remained the same regardless.

Though American values and culture made a deep impression on New York's East European Jewish immigrants, the Americans they met most often were Jews, particularly those of German ancestry, the so-called Yahudim. One might perhaps have expected Moses Weinberger to have scorned these Yahudim, particularly those among them who were prominent Reform Jews. Yet overall, *Jews and Judaism in New York* portrays uptown Jewry in remarkably favorable terms: "When it comes to charity, righteousness, and good deeds we cannot deny them their due. We may not hide the truth: in this respect they are better than we are—ten times better." More than most of his fellow East European Jewish immigrants, Weinberger realized that German-Jewish charity helped sustain the immigrant masses. As aloof and contemptuous as the Yahudim may have been, their actions spoke louder than words. They created an empire of benevolent institutions and invited East European Jews to exploit it for all it was worth. To be sure, many Yahudi institutions lacked sensitivity to immigrants' religious needs. For their part many of the immigrants responded ungratefully to all that had been done for them. But these clashes did not blind Weinberger to more fundamental underlying achievements. In the future, he hoped, immigrants would be more generous in their charity, and benevolent institutions more accommodating in their religious policies. Cooperation rather than separation was the goal he advocated.[13]

Considering Weinberger's strong opposition to religious reform, his cooperative stance seems surprising. He feared, after all, that innovators would make "everything lofty, holy and sublime" into "one everlasting ruin." Though he realized that Conservative Jews and Reform Jews differed—by 1887 the distinctions were institutionalized—he felt that "all the new parties have the same value, only two or three inches separate them." One innovation, he warned, would simply lead to another. Nothing would remain in the end. Until that awful moment, however, he would not break off ties. Even the men he condemned as "the leading sectarians" were still only "*almost* totally over the line." Something Jewish remained to be nurtured. Weinberger apparently realized that for the sake of Jewish survival, communal divisions had to be subordinated to the overarching attachment of peoplehood. Disunity was a luxury Jews could not afford.

The only people Weinberger wrote out of Judaism—"they are no longer part of us and have stopped being Jews"—were radical extremists ("Nihilists"). His opposition to them stemmed precisely from what he considered to be their lack of ethnic feeling: "they want to provoke disputes between men and their brothers." Their actions led him to doubt that "even one drop of ancestral blood . . . flowed in their veins." A Jew would not endanger another Jew's survival. Weinberger's vehemence likely stemmed from the aftermath of the 1886 Chicago

Haymarket riot, where an anarchist's bomb resulted in many dead and injured, leading to a wave of American nativism.[14] He understandably felt that Jews had to distance themselves from outsiders such as those who could prove so dangerous. By contrast, the threat posed by non-Orthodox Jews, serious as in his view it may have been, was at least internal. That in itself made it far less frightening.

Weinberger never assumed that all uptown Jews belonged to the Reform movement; that misconception only developed later. He knew that a conspicuous Orthodox community persisted uptown. Distant as he was from it geographically and socially, he gloried in its existence. He boasted to a foreign friend that a synagogue "whose members are enormously wealthy and completely German" held a daily afternoon Torah class. He heaped high praise on uptown Jewish elementary schools. He thought that J. P. Solomon's Orthodox *Hebrew Standard* was the finest Anglo-Jewish newspaper in New York. Weinberger did not mention but probably knew that Breslau-born Philip Joachimsen (1817–90), a respected New York lawyer and one of the Jewish community's foremost leaders, was Orthodox. So was the Berlin-born Henry Chuck (1829–90), a prosperous Sabbath-observant New York merchant who played an active role in the Beth Hamedrash Hagodol synagogue, the Machzike Talmud Thora yeshiva, and the appointment of Chief Rabbi Jacob Joseph.[15] These men, even if more numerous than generally imagined, only comprised a small minority element of New York Jewry. For immigrating Orthodox Jews, however, they served as valuable role-models and important sources of support.

Ties to other New York Jews notwithstanding, *Jews and Judaism in New York* devotes the bulk of its attention to traditionalist East European immigrant Jews, the people with whom Weinberger maintained most of his day-to-day contacts. Unsurprisingly the author first cast his eye over East Side religious life. That to him was of paramount importance.

From a purely numerical standpoint, Jewish religious life thrived in New York: synagogues numbered in the hundreds. On a deeper level, however, Weinberger perceived a host of troubling problems. Sometimes he merely described them: ignorance, arrogance, ritual laxity, unethical behavior, and so on. At other times he looked for scapegoats: natives, synagogue officers, boorish immigrants, even irreligious women. From his perspective he could not see that traditional immigrant Judaism itself was changing. Newcomers had begun the process that would transform East European Judaism into Judaism with an American flavor.

Already we have noted two aspects of this process: the movement from inner- to outer-directed Judaism, and the shift from a contemplative culture centered around study to a political one where power predominated. Slowly other kinds of changes took place as well. Weinberger noticed them; he could not have foreseen their implications.

First came the famous "edifice complex," the mania for ever larger and more splendid synagogues. The most important and wealthiest synagogues on the East Side—the Beth Hamedrash Hagodol, Ohab Zedek, Bene Israel "Kalwarier," and others—all erected enormous new structures in the mid-1880s, at a total cost of more than a quarter-million dollars. Weinberger properly pointed out that these new "palaces" greatly exceeded the needs of their existing members, and caused them to bear an enormous burden of debt. The same money, he charged, could have worked harder had it been devoted to educational and charitable endeavors. But of course, it would then have been inner-directed action, rather than outer-directed. Weinberger's suggestion would not have suited the needs of the day. The great shift from *stiebl* (a traditional small house of prayer) to showpiece was a transformation born of Judaism's confrontation with the world around it. East European Jewish immigrants, like their Jewish predecessors in America, wanted synagogues that they could proudly show off: both to Jews from other backgrounds and to Christian visitors.[16]

Ultimately all Jews benefited from the large Orthodox edifices. They raised immigrant self-esteem, and even brought East Europeans some of the outside respect they so sedulously sought. By building modern ostentatious structures, newcomers demonstrated their Americanization. They could engage in the same conspicuous consumption as everybody else. More important, the large new buildings led synagogue officials to enlarge their own frames of vision. They now had vast new expenses and required equally vast memberships. No longer could they afford just to appeal to *landsmen*. Instead they had to welcome East Europeans from different homelands into their midst. They had to begin to cater to more varied religious needs. They had to become more tolerant of different customs and traditions. As a result synagogues unconsciously joined with schools, newspapers, and Gentiles in ethnicizing Jews. By joining Jews together into a more solidly unified community, they helped them to forget their old destructive internal divisions.[17]

The second great innovation that Weinberger lamentingly described was the so-called *chazan*-craze. It began in 1886 when the Beth Hamedrash Hagodol advertised for a cantor in Europe and brought over Israel Michalovsky of Paris at a salary of $4,000. Subsequently one East Side congregation after another followed suit, importing the most famous European *chazanim* at ever higher salaries. Generally, the *chazanim* proved to be sound investments. They raised far more in tickets sales than they cost. Rabbis, Weinberger among them, lamented that cantorial extravaganzas frequently engendered violations of Jewish Sabbath laws, but they also knew that they filled up normally empty synagogues. The performances continued as long as demand for them remained high.

Contemporaries explained the *chazan*-craze in economic terms. The performances helped financially strapped synagogues meet their debt payments; they were roughly akin to modern-day bingo. This fails to explain, however, why East Side Jews found the *chazanim* so attractive and treated them with more veneration than they had in Europe. Weinberger described how a recently arrived immigrant spent his entire savings on a ticket, and how policemen were required to control the crowds seeking entry. Clearly, cantorial recitals met some deep-seated immigrant need.[18]

What the *chazan* represented, I think, was the ultimate synthesis of the Old World and New—a synthesis most immigrants sought to achieve but few succeeded. The *chazan* was an ideal role-model: observant yet rich, traditional yet modern. He formed a bridge between East Europe and the East Side. He personified the great heritage of a European world-gone-by, yet succeeded equally well in Columbus's land of the future. In short, a cantorial performance simultaneously served both as an exercise in nostalgia and as living proof that in America the talented could succeed handsomely. Immigrants considered the experience well worth paying for.

Once they came here, *chazanim* became a permanent fixture in East European showpiece congregations. This was hardly an American innovation; *chazanim* filled similar slots in Europe. As Weinberger points out, however, most East Side synagogues had previously depended on simple *baale tefilah*, congregational members who knew the appropriate chants and rejoiced at the opportunity to pour out their hearts before God. Professional *chazanim* effectively curtailed these personal devotions. Their arrival inaugurated another phase of traditional immigrant Judaism's outward turn: the shift from participation to performance. Members of large synagogues gradually became objects: sung to, spoken to, and ordered about. Indecorous behavior—loud personal prayers, wild gesticulations, and friendly conversation—was banned. Everyone made a maximum effort to put on a good show for the outside.[19]

The same factors that help account for the rise of *chazanim*—the need to raise funds, the quest for role-models, and the move to performance-oriented ritual—help also to account for some of the other changes in synagogue life that Weinberger noticed. Traditional synagogue officials—rabbis and preachers in particular—received little respect and poor salaries in America. Their lives, as Weinberger knew from experience, were hard and bitter—worse than in Europe. In immigrant eyes these men were vestiges of the old world, "defenders of the faith" who refused to Americanize. They could not serve as role-models for they did not know how to perform in public. They offered immigrants neither nostalgia for the past nor hope for the future. Later rabbis like Bernard Drachman, Philip Klein, Bernard Revel, and a preacher like Hirsch Masliansky enjoyed far better success precisely because they broke from the traditional pattern.[20] They performed ably, understood the problems of their day, and won the respect of outsiders. Their compensation and status rose accordingly.

The diminution of the rabbi's role in the 1880s led unsurprisingly to a corresponding rise in the status of laymen. They gave their services free and resembled far more closely the immigrant ideal—success in two worlds at once. Weinberger's magnificent characterization of these men demonstrates the distance separating his world from theirs. In a short time they had become ugly—and obviously envied—Americans:

> In America one relies for everything on three laymen. They are found by inspecting everyone who displays haughtiness and greed, talks big, leaps forward to barge into other peoples' conversations, has a tall and handsome appearance, and can't speak gently to his fellow human beings. . . . He is placed at the head of the community, given a golden scepter, which in this country is in the shape of a mallet, and with it he rules his people; he is at once their ruler and judge.

The height, handsome appearance, outgoing demeanor, and golden scepter—externals that Weinberger found so ludicrous—were precisely the factors that made the lay leader a talented and respected performer. Here was a man Jews could, and did, display with pride.

Performance and display similarly led to the enormous growth of the *bar-mitsvah* ceremony, "celebrated here," Weinberger scorned, "as the greatest of holidays among our Jewish brethren." The *bar-mitsvah* boy only appeared to be the center of attention; what was important in fact was the "great reception," the distinguished guests, and the "wisdom-filled speeches." These speeches often were delivered in English for the benefit of outsiders.Their words emphasized, in addition to traditional platitudes about becoming "a Jew equal to all Jews," that the *bar-mitsvah* boy should be "a good and honest citizen," "an honor to his nation, an honor to his country." From a simple rite of passage, the *bar-mitsvah* had grown into a public affirmation of the American Jewish faith.[21].

This transformation, like the others that Weinberger witnessed on the East Side, parallels to a greater degree than generally recognized developments taking place among Reform and Conservative Jews. Outwardly directed Judaism, showpiece sanctuaries, and display performances evidence in all three cases Judaism's confrontation with American culture. It was a confrontation no Jew could escape, it took place at many levels, and it affected all aspects of American Jewish life. Of course, every Jew had ultimately to find his own niche along the spectrum that stretched from completely traditional identification to thoroughgoing assimilation. Different synagogues and movements offered different compromises, and some proved more popular than others. But the tension implicit in the term "American Jew" was one that natives, Central European immigrants, and Eastern European immigrants all felt in common. No matter what they thought of the outside world, they had somehow to come to terms with it.

Moses Weinberger knew that Judaism in New York involved far more than just synagogue life. Casting his eyes upon the entire support system of Jewish life in the city—the complex of institutions and functionaries that made a life of piety possible—he discovered to his sorrow that it was changing as well. The problem as he saw it lay not in the lack of qualified personnel, for if anything there was a surfeit. Instead he blamed the deterioration on the decline of good Jewish values coupled with the too-ready acceptance of bad American ones.

The process of change displayed itself particularly starkly in the case of kosher meat. Traditional Jews eat meat only from certain biblically sanctioned animals, and then only if it is properly slaughtered and prepared. This serves both to reinforce Jewish group consciousness and to keep Jews apart from their nonkosher neighbors. In all major Jewish settlements, Jews have created their own kosher meat industry, with slaughtering, processing, and selling all done under their own carefully inspected auspices. Negligence, often compounded by efforts to cover it up, caused *kashrus* scandals throughout Jewish history. Since kosher meat is significantly more expensive than nonkosher meat, but often indistinguishable to the eye, tremendous temptation has always existed to substitute the one for the other so as to reap attendant profits. Piety and fear of disclosure, however, have generally prevented widespread abuse, especially in small towns where, to quote Weinberger, "every stone had seven eyes." But in New York these constraints did not work. Instead a business-oriented industry developed, described by one historian as a mixture of "fraud, corruption and holiness."[22]

Jews and Judaism in New York describes the sad state of New York *kashrus* in considerable detail. It blames some problems on state laws, others on crowded conditions, still others on incompetence. Moses Weinberger knew, however, that the root of the problem lay deeper. There was, first of all, no community control. In an atmosphere where disclosures, charges, and rumors abounded, fear of scandal became meaningless. Nobody was above suspicion, so everyone bought wherever he chose. In addition many of those involved in *kashrus* saw it as only another American business. Money to them became more important than piety. Like some secular merchants of their day, they argued that the buyer should beware. The biggest problem in *kashrus* regulation, however, was that many people, even if outwardly adherent, had lost their belief. Fear of sin no longer motivated them. Weinberger describes New York butchers who shamelessly sold nonkosher meat as kosher on the argument that their customers "are not among the scrupulous and could not care less." His own survey of immigrant practice confirmed the butchers' estimation: "a pile of bones and a large piece of spleen is more important to [a Jewish woman here] than the *kashrus* of the butcher and the meat in his store put together." For many East European Jewish immigrants the stature of *kashrus* had thus already declined from sacred rite to lax ritual. Pressure from the outside world coupled with considerations of convenience and economy soon led to even further decline. An increasing number of Jews abandoned *kashrus* entirely.[23]

Like *kashrus,* marriage and circumcision demand Jewish functionaries who, while not necessarily part of the synagogue, are required for proper ritual performance. The *mohel* who performs circumcisions must have special training; the marriage officiator needs a rudimentary knowledge of Jewish law. In New York, Weinberger found that the religious concerns of both these functionaries stood considerably below their pecuniary concerns: "They are merchants just like everybody else, only their merchandise is a circumcision and a marriage certificate." Like most merchants, their success depended on their Americanization:

> A *mohel* or marriage officiator here must be conscious of the world around him and the work ahead of him. He must know how to drive a chariot properly, how to select sure-footed horses, and how to find two or three of those transient characters known as *nosei kelim* [armor-bearers]. He must understand that nothing is more valuable or useful in America than smooth talk and vulgarity. He must realize that in New York, unlike the rest of the world, one spends even what one doesn't have. He who thoroughly understands all this may be sure of a place in this world: he will gather great riches, and never find himself without means of support.

Weinberger pointed to a half-dozen cases where "reverends," the title assumed by many of these functionaries, had flagrantly violated Jewish law in executing their "duties": sometimes out of ignorance, sometimes out of greed. He urged that performance of circumcisions and marriages be restricted, as in other countries, only to rabbis. The "horribly injurious and terribly destructive damage wrought by the anarchy that currently reigns among the Jews in this city," he wrote, demanded nothing less.[24]

In his opposition to lax East Side marriage practices, Weinberger unknowingly seconded complaints voiced by uptown Jews. They also expressed alarm over illegal and immoral actions by "self-appointed" ministers, and they insisted that something had to be done. In 1887, with the help of Jewish Assemblyman Jacob A. Cantor, they pushed a bill through the New York legislature, over immigrant opposition, that essentially limited eligibility to perform marriages to judges, justices of the peace, several government officials, and "ministers of legally incorporated religious congregations." Independent marriage brokers, unconnected with any society or *landsmanschaft,* were barred from the field.[25] While Weinberger's specific comments on this bill are not preserved, the fact that his views coincided with those of uptown leaders is highly significant. The rabbi for religious reasons, and the uptowners for secular ones, both sought in similar fashion to impose order on immigrant "anarchy." Precisely such kinds of temporary alliances—different, even opposing, groups supporting the same measures for different reasons—would later bring about passage of much-needed Progressive legislation.[26]

Legislation could only cure manifest symptoms of Jewish immigrant community problems; it ignored their underlying cause. That lay more deeply embedded in religion, for loss of faith had led to a collapse of immigrant values. Though Weinberger himself does not draw this conclusion, his bill of particulars certainly supports it. Ritual baths suffered from inadequate rabbinic inspection and insufficiently righteous bath attendants. Burial societies demonstrated insensitivity to impoverished members. Worst of all, Jews surrendered to despair and turned to begging. These beggars, Weinberger emphasized, were not the poor and unfortunate of the community. Instead he termed them cheaters and idlers: able-bodied people, undeserving of charity, whose outstretched hands deprived the truly indigent of their due.

The Danish immigrant Jacob Riis realized that beggary was at root a "moral distemper." "The pauper," he wrote, "is as hopeless as his own poverty."[27] Once these people would have been too proud to beg. They would have accepted their fate, increased their prayers, redoubled their efforts, and hoped for a better tomorrow. Conditions and values had changed, however, both in Europe and in America. Adrift in a world they did not understand, beggars unconsciously caricatured the morality they saw around them. Others worked hard for money; these people worked hard for it too. Others cast off traditional values; so did they.

Moses Weinberger termed immigrant Jewish beggars "a disgrace to all Israel." He might also have called them a Jewish tragedy. In the space of a few short months, these people had lost their homelands, their faith, and their shame. They were left rudderless, struggling to survive on wits alone. Their plight was worse than that of the average immigrant, but the difference was one of degree, not kind. They represented an extreme form of the social and spiritual crisis that pervaded the American Jewish immigrant community in general.

From Moses Weinberger's perspective, the home life of the East European Jewish immigrants lay in the same unsettled state as their communal life. America had disrupted a traditional balance between work, study, and leisure, between time spent away from home and time spent at home. It seemed to demand a new attitude to life, a new approach to home religion, a new relationship of man to wife, and a new way of raising children. Where once Judaism had regulated home life, in Weinberger's New York nothing seemed to regulate it at all.

Weinberger placed much of the blame for the immigrants' sad plight on their basic struggle to survive: "If they don't save themselves on the strength of their own blood, sweat, and tears . . . then they'll be lost forever." Many of the workers he described had never worked with their hands before. They joined the proletariat only in America. Suddenly they had to "spend all their time toiling." Their only joy in the world was "a place to revive."

Apparently, immigrants did not revive in the house of study. They "abandoned their Torah only from necessity—much against their will," Weinberger claimed, but he had earlier pointed out that power had become Jews' central goal and pastime. Instead of learning, the learned attended meetings. The only person to open the synagogues' book cabinets, he said, was "a poor visitor not yet enlightened as to the ways of New York." Everyone else was too concerned with livelihood and politics to follow the tradition of setting special times aside for study. Even neo-Hebraists, the young Jewish intellectuals of Eastern Europe, "turned their backs" and concentrated on the "nitty-gritty of existence." People remembered only what they learned in the old country, before they came.[28]

This picture of America as a spiritual wilderness where learning was neglected and books hard to find recurs frequently in Jewish writings of the nineteenth century. Orthodox and Reform Jews agreed: in America, to quote Isaac Mayer Wise, "ignorance swayed the scepter and darkness ruled."[29] It comes therefore as somewhat of a surprise to read in Weinberger's appended letter to a Hungarian friend that in America "many are excellent scholars who set aside special times for Torah study. . . . Among our Russian and Polish brothers we see this in almost every large congregation." Weinberger even found daily Torah study going on "uptown," among German Jews, something other sources confirm.[30] The contradiction between the former report and this one is manifest, but easily resolved: immigrants, like most people, varied their messages depending on their audience. The Weinberger who sought both to prevent scholars from immigrating and to bring about necessary reforms painted a dark picture of Jewish learning. When, however, he aimed to offer encouragement and reassurance, or to defend the land that he now called his own, he gave his words a more uplifting tone.[31] In truth there was greater learning in America than European Jews believed, but less than they were accustomed to at home. Traditional values and practices were deteriorating, but immigrant Jews had by no means abandoned them altogether.

A similar picture unfolds from Weinberger's scattered discussions of Sabbath and holiday observances. In the body of his text he refers to butchers who go to the marketplace on the Sabbath; ritual functionaries who "are not at all scrupulous about the laws of the Sabbath—the prohibitions on carrying, handling forbidden items, and conducting business," and synagogues that abet Sabbath violations connected with cantorial performances. Yet in his letter he paints the same situation in somewhat more balanced fashion. He still lists the violations; he prefaces them, however, with an important caveat: "with regard to the Sabbath . . . tranquility compares favorably to that found in most Jewish areas."

Festival observances formed a more serious problem, since for reasons of livelihood many chose to "open their stores on the holidays . . . especially on the second day." At the same time, however, observance of some festival-related commandments rose—building *sukos* (tabernacles), purchasing *lulavim* (palm branches) and *esrogim* (citrons) needed for the same holiday, and preparing specially inspected *matsos* (unleavened bread) for Passover. Traditionally observant New York Jews were searching for a middle ground between their Judaism and their jobs. In their home observance, as in other aspects of their life, they sought to balance identity and assimilation. So they floundered, continuing to cherish some aspects of Judaism even as they abandoned others with impunity.

These uncertainties placed a heavy strain on Jewish marriages. Domestic expectations of husbands and wives had to adapt to the changing circumstances of America. Frequently they could not. "Bills of divorce," Weinberger observed, "are very common."[32] Some men grew apart from their wives because they emigrated at different times and, when reunited, found themselves in different worlds. Weinberger mentioned the case of one man who was resigned to make peace with American norms, but his wife wasn't. She "felt most distressed and argued with him daily." On the other hand, there were women who, on Jewish holidays, "bustle[d] about from store to store, large baskets on their arms," even as their husbands were "joyfully sitting before God in the house of study." Neither tradition nor change was the exclusive preserve of either sex; the tension between the two worlds affected men and women equally. The demands of work likewise disrupted family life. Weinberger found men toiling too hard "to enjoy the delights of mankind. . . . All their lusts and cravings have left them." Leaving their wives neglected, many men spent most of their waking hours away from home.[33]

Naturally these domestic problems affected immigrant children. In the case of sons (the book ignores daughters), Weinberger found that values which fathers had traditionally impressed upon them at home—particularly education and piety—remained untaught. "Instead of training their sons to follow in their ways," he charged, fathers "spend their time inspecting . . . synagogue officials." Of course, he realized that the situation was actually more complicated. In some homes both parents worked. Other children were orphaned. Not a few became unruly vagrants at a shockingly young age. But these cases aside, many parents refrained from teaching traditional values because they no longer felt sure of them themselves. They knew that a child "must learn to establish for himself a goal in life, and become familiar with the ways of the world." For that they sent their children to public schools. They so little valued Jewish education, however, that it became a poorly paid, "scorned and debased profession." No sooner did a child reach the magic age of thirteen than he abandoned his Jewish education altogether and began to pursue "lucre, a life of pleasure, and all human gratifications," abandoning completely his "faith, Torah, and holy roots."

Weinberger's picture of Jewish education is fascinatingly different from that painted by social workers and professional educators.[34] They worried about the miserably delapidated condition of schoolrooms, many of them unfit for habitation; the untrained teachers who used "medieval forms of schooling," seemingly inappropriate to American conditions; the overall lack of administrative organization and control in Jewish education; and the large numbers of children who received no Jewish education at all. Weinberger, on the other hand, worried about teachers' poor salaries, their difficulty in finding work, the lack of support they received from parents, and the frustrations they suffered teaching students so terribly inferior to those found in Eastern Europe. These divergent outlooks reflect more than mere differences of focus, more even than just normal disagreements between professionals and non-professionals. They rather symbolize the clash between two world-views: one of American-trained educators, the other of European traditionalists. Immigrant Jewish families, children in particular, found themselves caught in the middle.

Based upon what he saw in New York—changes in the synagogue, a deteriorating communal structure, and unsettled Jewish homes—Moses Weinberger expressed understandable fear for the future. He had "no hope at all" that children would follow in the way of Torah. How could they with the minimal education they received? Religious innovations, which some viewed optimistically, appeared to him to be leading Jews straight to "ruin." The expensive cantors and palatial synagogues might bankrupt the community, but he doubted that they would improve what the Publisher's Preface called "our terribly degenerate spiritual situation." The only bright spots in the whole bleak picture were "conservative reforms," those aimed at restoring time-tested values and practices. The establishment in New York of a talmudic academy based on traditional principles, Yeshivas Ets Chayim, was one such hopeful development.[35] Weinberger considered it a "marvelous thing—a wonder," so wonderful in fact that it seemed to him almost too good to be true. He similarly found encouragement in the growth of Jewish bookstores, and the increased observance of some holiday rituals. "Perhaps there is hope," he suggested at one point. "Destruction" could still be averted.

Weinberger, like many Jewish leaders before him, cherished his own ambitious plan to revitalize the spiritual condition of New York Jews. He promised to set forth its full details in a separate volume (which never appeared). But to avoid delay, and perhaps to whet the appetite of his readers, he offered a bare, four-part outline of his proposal in the final pages of his narrative.

1. Unification. New York should have a total of no more than ten or twelve synagogues.
2. Association. The twelve congregations should work together as a communal body.
3. Appointment of rabbis. Every congregation should be headed by a competent, recognized spiritual leader.
4. Creation of a chief rabbinate or Jewish Supreme Court.

In one sense these reforms were in tune with the best Progressive ideas of the day. They stressed efficiency, rationalization, discipline, and leadership—all aimed at creating order from seeming chaos.[36] Some of these same ends lay behind the creation of the Central Conference of American Rabbis by Reform Jewish leaders at about the same time. On the other hand, these were profoundly conservative reforms. Weinberger proposed to give over all power to "competent" rabbis. He offered no semblance of democracy, and no leadership role at all to laymen.[37] Indeed he scorned a lay initiative already underway aimed at appointing just the kind of chief rabbi he proposed. He predicted—quite wrongly as it turned out—that the much-discussed initiative would fail. Only rabbis, he thought, had the proper qualifications to carry out such ambitious undertakings.

The initiative in fact succeeded handsomely; it was the chief rabbi,

Jacob Joseph, who failed. Voluntarism religious freedom, denominationalism, and church-state separation—hallmarks of American religion—would probably have prevented effective religious rule by any
central Jewish leader. In this case, when conflicts arose, the chief rabbi
found himself powerless and alone.[38] Even in Europe, Jewish unity and
rabbinical control existed more in dream than reality. In America, where
the "great tradition of the American churches" militated against this kind
of religious discipline, proposals such as Weinberger's were doomed
from the start. Conservative reforms—everything from strict Sabbath
observance to rabbinical courts to advanced yeshivahs—could be effectuated in America, and in time they were. But first the "old wine" had
to be packaged in new bottles—ones distinctively American in appearance and form.[39]

Moses Weinberger's readers seem to have paid little attention to his
proposed solutions. They read *Jews and Judaism in New York* for its
descriptions and pronounced them to be basically accurate. Ephraim
Deinard, the cantankerous bibliophile and Hebraist, thought that Weinberger's portrait fitted all big cities in America—"it will serve as trustworthy guide for those writing the history of Jews in the New World."
Max Raisin, though a Reform rabbi, agreed: "one researching the roots
of Russian Jewry in this great city will find in this volume considerable
material." Perhaps contemporary reviewers considered Weinberger's
suggestions at great length, but if so their reviews have been forgotten.
Those newspapers that I examined ignored Weinberger completely.
According to Jacob Zausmer, *Jews and Judaism in New York* did cross the
Atlantic for he read it before emigrating. Apparently, however, European Jews paid Weinberger no more heed than they paid their own
rabbis. As conditions in Eastern Europe worsened, and reports of
economic opportunity in America grew, Jews emigrated. For many, strict
observance of Judaism took on a lower priority than survival and
success.[40]

Ironically, the same immigrant flow that Weinberger attempted to
slacken led indirectly to his first rabbinical position. In the fall of 1890, a
full decade after he arrived in America and three years after *Jews and
Judaism in New York* appeared, he assumed the position of rabbi and *av bes
din* (chief judge) at Congregation Bnai Israel Anshai Ungarin in Scranton,
Pennsylvania. From there his career for a short while took on the appearance of a Horatio Alger tale of success. In 1891 he was invited to
inaugurate the new sanctuary of the Hungarian congregation, Ohaw

Sholom, in Philadelphia. By 1893 he had become that congregation's full-time rabbi. Two years later he bettered himself again. The Hungarian Congregation Beth Hamedrash Hagodol on Willett Street—the New York congregation where he had been active before assuming the Scranton post—invited him to return to serve as its rabbi and *av bes din.* On May 12, 1895, the Jewish holiday of Lag Ba'omer and by coincidence his birthday, he delivered his maiden address to this congregation. Most appropriately, he took as his text the famous words of King David: "What am I, O Lord God, and what is my family, that You have brought me thus far?" (2 Samuel 7:18).[41]

The young King David, in his subsequent career, fully justified the faith placed in him. Moses Weinberger proved less fortunate. His subsequent rabbinical career illustrates many of the problems that immigrant Orthodox rabbis faced in America. Underpaid by his congregation, he had continually to seek employment on the side: teaching, performing religious functions, or engaging in unrelated businesses, which ultimately led him into conflict. He also became involved in bitter disputes over *kashrus.* Unlike many of his colleagues, he did not become financially dependent on the kosher food industry. But he did become involved in its problems when rabbinic questions were posed to him. At least in his published responsa, he repeatedly supported *shochatim* against charges of unfitness seemingly motivated more by personal and economic factors than by religious ones. This stance, of course, brought him into open conflict with rabbis sympathetic to slaughterers' unions. He pressed on regardless. Old dreams of Orthodox unity gave way before the realities of divergent interests.[42]

Finally, Weinberger faced constant opposition from among his congregation's dissatisfied—and to his mind unqualified—laymen. Where he lay stress on traditional learning, devoted his energies to the formation of a Jewish Rabbinical High School (founded October 1895), and expended many hours on scholarly writings, these congregants sought a rabbi who would concern himself with image, growth, and development. Openly scornful of Weinberger's educational efforts, they sought to redirect congregational activities outward. They wanted to buy a new synagogue and to attract new members. If that meant discarding a few time-honored traditions, they were prepared to pay the price.

For eleven years Weinberger kept his position, frequent quarrels and his own difficult economic plight notwithstanding. In August 1905 a dispute caused him to cut back on his classes, and some time later an effort was made to have him fired. But he had a contract and held on, calling all the while for reconciliation. Then on the last day of Passover, April 17, 1906, accumulated tensions finally exploded. The Hungarian Congregation Beth Hamedrash Hagodol erupted in rioting and police had to be called to quell the disturbance. The incident that occasioned the violence was Rabbi Weinberger's entry into the *matsah* business. He claimed to need extra money. This divided the congregation (some congregants were in the *matsah* business themselves), led to catcalling during the rabbi's Passover sermon, and finally resulted in blows being exchanged. In the aftermath, Rabbi Weinberger refused to resign his position, placed a ban on his synagogue, and never entered its premises again. Though later he sought reconciliation, he apparently spent his remaining years "in exile," producing *matsah*.[43]

On the surface, based on the limited data available, the Passover riot looks like a classic battle between traditionalists and innovators. Rabbi Weinberger stood for time-tested values; his opponents demanded change. But closer examination reveals a more complicated picture. Weinberger, by entering the *matsah* business, projected an entrepreneurial image far more characteristically American than Jewish. On the other hand, Weinberger's opponents, seemingly more outwardly oriented, righteously cloaked themselves in the mantle of tradition, opposing the rabbi's undertaking as both inappropriate and without precedent. Each side thus respected tradition and feared change, while both—albeit in different ways and for different reasons—also deviated from tradition and accepted change. The resulting guilt, anger, and confusion go far to explain the passionate violence that ensued. In rioting over Weinberger, immigrants partly expressed their frustration at the New World in general.

The process that transformed East European immigrant Judaism found expression in Weinberger's book and brought tumult to his congregation. Many details of the process have yet to be examined. Some of the generalizations suggested here, based on Weinberger's work, may not bear up under closer scrutiny.[44] Forces of tradition and change, however, certainly waged war on the East Side. Disputes over innovations continued long after *Jews and Judaism in New York* lay forgotten, for each new group of immigrants had to adjust afresh. Slowly new forms of Judaism took shape. In fashionable neighborhoods ("areas of third settlement"), as Marshall Sklare has shown, children of more successful immigrant families became Conservative Jews. Another new movement, now known as Modern Orthodoxy, also evolved. Both built showpiece

synagogues, concerned themselves with the outside world, adopted performance-oriented rituals, and displayed thorough tolerance for non-
observant Jews who sought affiliation.[45] Weinberger, back in 1887, saw
many of these changes coming. He held little hope for Judaism as he
knew it. But overall he was too pessimistic. Though it adapted to many
demands of the modern world, Judaism managed to maintain its identity, mediating the tension between tradition and change. The Judaism of
today's New York certainly would not please Moses Weinberger, but his
angry scowl might soften into an expression of bewildered surprise. For
however much the state of Jews and Judaism in New York has evolved
over time, the community as a whole—and American Jewry as well—still
remains religiously vibrant.

Notes

1.   Except where otherwise noted, all quotations and information in this
Introduction derive directly from *Jews and Judaism in New York*.

2.   Judah David Eisenstein, *Ozar Zikhronothai* (New York, 1929), p. 45.

3.   For various accounts of New York Jewry and American Orthodoxy
during this period, see Eisenstein, *Ozar Zikhronothai;* Max Raisin, *Leaves from a
Rabbi's Notebook* (Hebrew; New York, 1941), pp. 165–190; Zvi Hirsch Bernstein,
"A Few Words on Jews and Judaism Thirty-Four Years Ago in New York" (in
Hebrew), *Yalkut Maarabi*, 1 (1904): 128–34; Peter Wiernik, *History of Jews in America*
(New York, 1972 [1931]), pp. 179–92, 250–59; Moshe Davis, *Beit Yisrael Be-
Amerikah* (Jerusalem, 1970), pp.31–66; Moses Rischin, *The Promised City* (New
York, 1962); Charles S. Liebman, "Religion, Class and Culture in American
Jewish History," *Jewish Journal of Sociology* 9 (December 1967): 227–42; and Jo
Renee-Fine and Gerald R. Wolfe, *The Synagogues of New York's Lower East Side* (New
York, 1978), pp. 25–66.

4.   Abraham J. Karp, "New York Chooses a Chief Rabbi, "*Publications of
the American Jewish Historical Society* 44(1954): 129–98; Judah M. Isaacs, "Abraham
Jacob Gerson Lesser," in Leo Jung (ed.), *Guardians of Our Heritage* (New York,
1955), pp. 347–59.

5.   *Hebrew Standard,* April 27, 1906, p. 8; Moses Weinberger, *Rosh Divre
Mosheh* (Philadelphia, 1895), pp. 9–10; Weinberger, *Dorosh Dorash Mosheh* (New
York, 1914), pp. 30–39.

6.   Brief biographies of Weinberger in Eisenstein, *Ozar Zikhronothai*
p. 191; Getzel Kressel, *Cyclopedia of Modern Hebrew Literature* 1 (Hebrew; Merhavia,
1965): 657; and Ben-Zion Eisenstadt, *Israel Scholars in America* (Hebrew; New York,
1903), p. 40, are incomplete and contain minor inaccuracies. I have relied on
scattered evidence found in Weinberger's collected writings. See also *American
Hebrew*, 38 (April 12, 1889): 160–61.

7.   *Machzike Talmud Thora* (New York, 1885); *Jewish Messenger,* April 16,
1886, p. 2 and November 11, 1887, p. 2; Richard Wheatley, "The Jews In New
York," *Century Magazine* 43 (February 1892): 519; Raisin, *Leaves from a Rabbi's
Notebook,* p. 178; Alexander M. Dushkin, *Jewish Education in New York City* (New

York, 1918), pp. 69–71 and passim; Jeremiah J. Berman, "Jewish Education in New York City 1860–1900," *Yivo Annual of Jewish Social Science* 9 (1954): 253, 272–75; Judah Pilch (ed.), *A History of Jewish Education in America* (New York, 1969), p. 49; and the somewhat inaccurate account reprinted in Allon Schoener, *Portal to America* (New York, 1967), pp. 108–9.

    8.   See also Weinberger, *Dorosh Dorash Mosheh,* pp. 46–55.

    9.   Weinberger's comments were in marked contrast to earlier optimistic messages sent by immigrants calling on European Jews to join them in the New World. See Davis, *Beit Yisrael Be-Amerikah,* pp. 34–35.

    10.   See Randall M. Miller and Thomas D. Marzik (eds.), *Immigrants and Religion in Urban America* (Philadelphia, 1977).I concern myself in what follows mainly with Weinberger's perceptions, and only occasionally with whether or not they were accurate. For comparable portraits, see Gershon Rosenzweig, *Masechet Amerika* (Vilna, 1894); and more broadly, Shlomo Noble, "The Image of the American Jew in Hebrew and Yiddish Literature in America, 1870–1900," *Yivo Annual* 9 (1954): pp. 83–108.

    11.   See also Weinberger, *Dorosh Dorash Mosheh,* pp. 97, 120.

    12.   See Alexander Harkavy's description of a traveling *"mitsvah* merchant" in his *Prakim Mechayai* (New York, 1935), p. 62; translated in *American Jewish Archives* 33 (April 1981), p. 51.

    13.   Zosa Szjakowski, "The Yahudi and the Immigrant: A Reappraisal," *American Jewish Historical Quarterly (AJHQ)* 63 (September 1973): 13–44.

    14.   John Higham, *Strangers in the Land* (New York, 1973): 54–57.

    15.   On Joachimsen, see *Encyclopedia Judaica* 10 (1972): 110; Wheatley, "Jews in New York," p. 526; Eisenstein, *Ozar Zikhronothai,* pp. 65, 257; and on Chuck, ibid., p. 268.

    16.   Compare Leon Jick, *The Americanization of the Synagogue, 1820–1870* (Hanover, N.H., 1976), pp. 178–81.

    17.   See Weinberger, *Dorosh Dorash Mosheh,* pp. 96–97; Rischin, *Promised City,* p. 105; Jonathan D. Sarna, "From Immigrants to Ethnics: Toward a New Theory of 'Ethnicization,'" *Ethnicity* 5 (1978): 370–78.

    18.   *Jewish Messenger,* September 3, 1886; September 17, 1886; September 23, 1887; *American Hebrew,* August 13, 1886, p. 9; Eisenstein, *Ozar Zikhronothai,* p. 251.

    19.   Smaller Orthodox synagogues resisted this trend. For a present-day portrait, see Samuel C. Heilman, *Synagogue Life* (Chicago, 1976).

    20.   Bernard Drachman, *The Unfailing Light: Memoirs of an American Rabbi* (New York, 1948); Aaron Rothkoff, *Bernard Revel: Builder of American Jewish Orthodoxy* (Philadelphia, 1972); Z. H. Masliansky, *Memoirs and Travels* (Hebrew; New York, 1929), pp. 161–217; Eugene Markovitz, "Henry Pereira Mendes: Architect of the Union of Orthodox Jewish Congregations of America," *AJHQ* 55 (March 1966), pp. 364–84.

    21.   Quotations are from *The Jewish American Orator* (New York, 1928), pp. 40, 59; see also Rosenzweig, *Masechet Amerika,* p. 23; and more broadly, Isaac Rivkind *Bar Mitzvah* (Hebrew; New York, 1942), esp. pp. 62–64.

    22.   Jeremiah J. Berman, *Shehitah* (New York, 1941); Harold P. Gastwirt, *Fraud, Corruption and Holiness* (New York, 1974); cf. Schoener, *Portal to America,* pp. 112–15.

    23.   Compare Stephen A. Speisman, *The Jews of Toronto* (Toronto, 1979), pp. 279–83; Sidney Goldstein and Calvin Goldscheider, *Jewish Americans* (Englewood Cliffs, N.J., 1968), pp. 195–204.

24.   Rosenzweig, *Masechet Amerika,* p. 32; Aaron Rothkoff, "The American Sojourn of Ridbaz," *AJHQ* 57 (1968): 563–64.

25.   *American Hebrew*, November 26, 1886, p. 38; March-April 1887; *Jewish Messenger,* September 17, 1886, p. 6; February 25, 1887, p. 3; *New York Herald*, March 27, 1887, p. 20.

26.   J. Joseph Huthmacher, "Urban Liberalism and the Age of Reform," *Mississippi Valley Historical Review* 44 (September 1962): 231–41; John D. Buenker, *Urban Liberalism and Progressive Reform* (New York, 1973).

27.   Jacob Riis, *How the Other Half Lives* (New York, 1957 [1890]), p. 186.

28.   Compare Samuel B. Schwarzberg, *Tichtov Zot Ledor Acharon* (New York, 1898).

29.   Isaac M. Wise, *Reminiscences* (Cincinnati, 1901), p. 148; Gershom Greenberg, "The Significance of America in David Einhorn's Conception of History," *AJHQ* 63 (December 1973): 162–63; Rosenweig, *Masechet Amerika,* esp. p. 29.

30.   Cf. Eisenstein, *Ozar Zikhronothai,* p. 11; Bernstein, "A Few Words," pp. 128–29.

31.   Immigrant letters to Europe frequently painted America in unrealistically bright colors. See, for example, Lois Rubin, "Disappointed Expectations: An Immigrant Arrives in Western Pennsylvania," *Western Pennsylvania Historical Magazine* 59 (October 1976): 451–52 and Abraham Cahan, *The Education of Abraham Cahan,* trans. Leon Stein et al. (Philadelphia, 1969), p. 242.

32.   Wheatley, "Jews in New York," p. 12; Rosenzweig, *Masechet Amerika,* p. 29; and Schoener, *Portal to America,* pp. 107–8, make the same point.

33.   Cf. Hutchins Hapgood, *The Spirit of the Ghetto* (New York, 1966 [1902]), pp. 76-90; for other views, see Maxine Seller, "Beyond the Stereotype: A New Look at the Immigrant Woman, 1880-1924," *Journal of Ethnic Studies* 3 (1975): 59–70; and Herbert G. Gutman, *Work, Culture and Society in Industrializing America* (New York, 1976), pp. 41–44.

34.   Lloyd P. Gartner, "The Jews of New York's East Side, 1890–1893," *AJHQ* 53 (1964): 264–84; Mordecai Kaplan and Bernard Cronson, "First Communal Survey of Jewish Education in New York City—1909, *Jewish Education* 20 (1949): 113–16; Dushkin, *Jewish Education,* pp. 63–99; 145–406.

35.   Gilbert Klaperman, *The Story of Yeshiva University* (New York, 1969), pp. 17–33.

36.   Robert H. Wiebe, *The Search for Order* (New York, 1967).

37.   For a different Orthodox approach to democracy and American values, see the neglected writings of Rabbi Chaim Hirschensohn, best summarized in Eliezer Schweid, *Democracy and Halakhah* (Hebrew; Jerusalem, 1978).

38.   Karp, "New York Chooses a Chief Rabbi"; Cahan, *The Education of Abraham Cahan,* pp. 394–96; Sydney E. Ahlstrom, *A Religious History of the American People* (New Haven, 1972), pp. 379–84.

39.   See William B. Helmreich, "Old Wine in New Bottles: Advanced Yeshivot in the United States," *American Jewish History* 69 (December 1979): 234–56. The other articles in this issue also deal with American Orthodox Judaism.

40.   Ephraim Deinard, *Koheleth Amerika* (St. Louis, 1925), p. 59; Raisin, *Leaves from a Rabbi's Notebook,* p. 375; Jacob Zausmer, *Footprints of a Generation* (New York, 1957), p. 208; cf. Eisenstein, *Ozar Zikhronothai,* p. 380.

41.   Weinberger, *Dorosh Dorash Mosheh,* pp. 1, 30, 46, 55, 88; Weinberger, *Kuntres Halachah Lemosheh* (Philadelphia, 1894); Weinberger, *Rosh Divre Mosheh* (Philadelphia, 1895).

42. Weinberger, *Kuntres Halachah Lemosheh;* Weinberger, *Kuntres Ho'il Mosheh* (New York, 1895); Weinberger, *Halachah Lemosheh* (New York, 1902); cf. Weinberger, *Igeret Mishneh* (New York, 1909), pp. 9–11, and Gastwirt, *Fraud, Corruption and Holiness,* pp. 77–81.

43. [M. Weinberger], *Torah Or* (New York, 1896); Weinberger, *Dorosh Dorash Mosheh,* esp. pp. 120ff.; *Divre Shalom Ve'emes* (New York, 1908); Weinberger, *Igeres Mishneh; New York Sun,* April 18, 1906, p. 5; April 22, 1906, p. 16; *Hebrew Standard*, April 27, 1906, p. 8; *Jewish Daily Bulletin,* December 10, 1930, p. 3. An obituary for Weinberger appears in the *New York Times,* June 14, 1940, p. 21.

44. On this adjustment process and the part religion played in it, see *inter alia,* Y. Jellinek, "The House of Prayer in the Life of the East European Immigrant in America, 1880–1920" (Hebrew), in Historical Society of Israel, *Hartsaot Bekinuse Ha'iyun Behistoriah* (Jerusalem, 1973), pp. 81–100; Victor Greene, *For God and Country* (Madison, Wis., 1975); and Timothy Smith, "Religion and Ethnicity in America," *American Historical Review* 83 (December 1978): 1155–85.

45. Marshall Sklare, *Conservative Judaism* (2nd ed.; New York, 1972); Ralph Pelcovitz, *Danger and Opportunity* (New York, 1976), pp. 11–68; Howard I. Levine, "The Non-Observant Orthodox," *A Treasury of Tradition,* ed. Norman Lamm and Walter S. Wurzburger (New York, 1967), pp. 118–37; Jerome E. Carlin and Saul H. Mendlovitz, "The American Rabbi: A Religious Specialist Responds to Loss of Authority," *The Jews,* ed. Marshall Sklare (New York, 1958), pp. 377–414; Solomon Poll, "The Persistence of Tradition: Orthodoxy in America," *The Ghetto and Beyond,* ed. Peter I. Rose (New York, 1969), pp. 118–49; Charles Liebman, "Orthodoxy in American Jewish Life," *American Jewish Year Book* 66 (1965): 21–97; Liebman, *The Ambivalent American Jew* (Philadelphia, 1973), pp. 42–87.

Moses Weinberger's
Jews and Judaism in New York

Publisher's Preface

"[The Torah] is a tree of life to all who hold fast to it" [Lamentations 5:2]. Had the text read "all who labor in it" there would have been no protection for anybody else. It therefore reads "hold fast to it" to include those who uphold its students (Midrash Tanchuma).

TO THE READER

From the directors and leaders of the Machzike Talmud Thora Society here in New York.

We lay before you, dear readers, this book: *Jews and Judaism in New York*. Its proceeds will be devoted to the Machzike Talmud Thora [Support of the Religious School] Society, 227 East Broadway, and it is written by a valuable and honorable man, author of many works, wise in all branches of knowledge, and ordained by the greatest rabbis in Hungary: the sharp-witted rabbi and *gaon*, eminent in Torah, piety and wisdom, our master, Rabbi Moses Weinberger, may his light shine forth.

As the reader will learn in this book, the subject that interests the author is a most valuable one, a matter of paramount concern to us, which to date has still not been sufficiently explored, although a great deal has been written about it. The distinguished author is not characteristically one who stands up reprovingly, telling men of their sins. He could nevertheless not observe with silence and complacency our terribly degenerate spiritual situation in this country, which seemingly grows worse from day to day, to such an extent that the bad now exceeds the good. In spite of this, nobody sounds the alarm to do something for the sake of our holy faith, to rebuild the wrecked altar of our religion. American Judaism croons like a dove bitterly mourning its humbled state. Fault lies with its blind leadership, who brought it down from a position of holiness and dressed it in a new garb—one of trade, splendor, pride, hatred, jealousy, competition, and similar ugly things that repel the honest Jewish soul.

As a consequence of this crisis, the author took it upon himself to investigate the position of our Jewish brethren who emigrated to this new land from the countries where they were dispersed. God having graciously granted him Torah, wisdom, knowledge, and skill, he has penetrated in this book to the very depths of the subject before us. What he brought up is a string of pearls, clear information and proper views that cast sharp light on the position of our Jewish brethren in this country and city: their material and ethical situation, customs and arrangements, comings and goings, manners and walks of life, and their religious ways; their synagogues, *chazanim* [cantors], rabbis, *mohalim* [ritual circumcisers], *shochatim* [ritual slaughterers], and *bodkim* [ritual inspectors] (?)[1] as well as all their other religious functionaries. He collected all this like a bundle of sheaves and laid it out in clear, reliable language, using proofs and examples that are incisive and irrefutable. He succeeds in a way in which no previous attempt has to uncover the origin of our dark situation, the means by which it may be repaired, and the method by which the great wall of religion against which all Israel rests can be fortified. In the book before him the reader will see remarks that are both apt and well arranged.

The author deserves special acclaim for having undertaken this book without any desire for reward. He turned not to the haughty and well-heeled who, with their money, purchase authors who then amuse their patrons with twisting dances of praise and lofty sketches designed for their pleasure. Such authors must frequently engage in hypocritical flattery, covering up sins and faults lest they provoke the very readers whom they aspire to reach. In this way truth is hidden, and books become completely fraudulent. Our friend, the author of this book, would have none of this! He refused to transform his book into a money-making venture. As we have said, any money he does make has been dedicated to our Machzike Talmud Thora Society. So righteous a man, it can easily be seen, will not be swayed by some flatterer to do as others bid or to take any position not in accordance with religious teaching. He thus achieved the essential purpose that he set out for himself in this book: the cause of truth and peace. His road is the road of holiness. We hope that his forceful words will stir the hearts of our Jewish brethren to improve their ways, that each person may labor individually to strengthen our religion and faith. May the Lord our God aid us in this— *Amen Selah.*

We have gone on long enough, if not too long, dear readers. It remains for us to tell you something about the coming expansion of our

Talmud Torah, and about the hardship that this hallowed work has entailed over these past four years. We admit unabashedly that at its birth the Talmud Torah was small, impoverished, and in very narrow quarters. The small scraps that we collected from those few members who supported the lofty project hardly satisfied that mighty lion—our expenditures. The need for an ambitious project like this in God's great city of New York is enormous; so too are the obstacles that stood in its path. More than once we worried that a shortage of money would preclude us from covering our deficit, and that all our work would be in vain. Nevertheless, we refused to submit to discouragement or fear. We rather marshaled our forces to improve and glorify the Talmud Torah in all possible ways. Finally, after a great deal of work and effort, we succeeded in substantially increasing the number of our members. This has yielded funds for the Talmud Torah's support, for each man gives us as much as his heart allows.

So our minds were made up: we set about building. Looking back now over the four years since we founded the Talmud Torah, we see that we moved ever forward, taking giant steps upward each time. With God's help, three years ago, we were able to lease a mansion on 83 East Broadway. It then became time for us to hire skilled teachers. A few months later, we increased their number to six, giving each one a separate class to himself. They went about their work successfully, with skill, faith, and ingenuity, making the Talmud Torah better from day to day. Now the great moment has arrived when we can improve it even more, increasing our supervision over the studies, the teachers, and the building—which serves as a standard for our Orthodox Jewish brethren in New York.

But hard times have fallen over this country. With our people unable to find work, the number of fathers daily knocking on our door asking us to place their sons in our Talmud Torah has increased greatly in the past year. They lack funds for instructors to teach their children knowledge and reverence of God. We have done all that we can, and more. We took many children into the Talmud Torah and gave them a place, though we became crowded and cramped, and this greatly interfered with studies. In the end, we saw no way to solve the problem except by leasing another building, larger than our first, which could hold even those youngsters whom we could not admit for lack of room, many of whom now wander around the streets of New York, getting into trouble. At about that time God awakened the spirit of our righteous president, the noble master and *gaon,* the eminent Rabbi Israel [Isidor] Rosenthal,[2] may his light shine forth, and his assistant, the eminent Rabbi Dov Kleif,[3] and they called a mass meeting last fall. In his gentle yet forceful way the honorable President Rosenthal stirred the hearts of our Jewish brethren to donate money to purchase a permanent home for the Talmud Torah, for so long as it is required to move from place to place it can never endure. He was as good as his word, removing from his pocket a $100 donation. Taking their cue from his example, many raised their donations. He then called other meetings, and ultimately succeeded in collecting a sum amounting to some $4,000. Still he refused to stop and rest, and sought constantly to do more and more. Finally he succeeded in purchasing for the Talmud Torah, at a price of $16,000, the mansion that stands on 227 East Broadway. But alas the amount collected was too small to cover the cost of the purchase, that is $8,000 down, and the rest to be paid after a certain set period. So our president again extended his hand, and provided a loan from his own pocket to make up the $8,000 down payment. A few months ago the purchase was signed and sealed. The deed is done.

We can now thank God Almighty who has kept us, sustained us, and brought us to the point where we can establish a building in Israel out of which the light of Torah can flow to the poor of our nation. This redounds to the glory of our Orthodox brethren in America for *can there possibly be a greater* mitsvah *or holier obligation than the teaching of Torah?* Indeed, so long as we have been in America, we have asked ourselves in sorrow: When will we be able to uphold this *mitsvah* and carry it out to completion? A *mitsvah,* after all is only credited to the one who completes it; so long as it remains incomplete, it cannot fulfill its true aim, and does not fall under the rubric of *mitsvah* at all. It is with some bitterness, therefore, that we must tell our Jewish brethren that our task remains unfinished. Before we can make a blessing over completion, the goal toward which we are working, we still need a great deal of money. Money, only money is the life force behind all that is attempted and accomplished in America. Means can achieve what the mind cannot. It should thus be easy to understand that a great, enlightened, and charitable project like this one cannot be built or completed without money. "With money shall he lay its foundation; with money shall he set up its gates" [see Joshua 6:26]. The money needed to complete the purchase of a building for the Talmud Torah lies not in the heavens where, it might be said, "Go and get it for me from there" [see Deuteronomy 30:12]. We must accomplish it on our own, and can do so only if our Jewish brethren will come forward with donations. Let each one hurry to contribute his shekel, giving as much as he likes or can so that we can progress without stopping, and congratulate ourselves on successfully completing our task. It is distressing to see our Jewish brethren downtown wasting their money on things of little value that merely provide them with momentary gratification, when this honorable and invaluable project will bring eternal spiritual joy and will be remembered forever. Brethren, do not forget that *a great* mitsvah *lies before you waiting to be performed.* You won't always be able to find one. By performing it, you can in a short time and at a very low price purchase a share in the world to come. It is therefore incumbent upon each and every Jew to come forward as soon as he can, for one should not let a *mitsvah* pass one by. Don't miss the chance to perform a *mitsvah* that comes your way. Do it at once! Everything is best at its proper time, especially a great *mitsvah* like Talmud Torah, which is equivalent to all other *mitsvos* in the Torah combined. Its fruits are enjoyed in this world; its capital reserved for the world to come [see Mishna Pe'ah 1:1]: spiritual life, eternal life, a life of joy amidst heavenly treasures whose value exceeds that of gold, silver, and precious objects—and all for the small price of a few shekels, as much as each person feels he can afford.

Should we not cover our faces in shame when we see our Orthodox Jewish brethren, who boast of their piety and religiosity, devoting their strength solely to the task of increasing the number of synagogues in Israel? When each congregation builds a separate sanctuary for itself and wastes money on small things, the absence of which, as any expert knows, would hardly be felt? Yet this is done at a time when the entire great city of New York, full as it is of Jews, can boast of but one single, lonely Talmud Torah of its kind; and this one, in spite of all the laborious efforts of its founders, has still not succeeded in freeing itself from creditors to stand independently on its own feet.

Let us investigate which of these two is more important: the synagogue or the Talmud Torah? We cannot deny that having a synagogue for holding prayers is a central principle basic to our religion. But important and holy as it is, this principle is completely overshadowed by the *mitsvah* of Talmud Torah. Our rabbis taught us that one should not neglect children's studies even in order to build the Temple. If for the Temple not, obviously not for the building of a synagogue! In our day, particularly, since we have more than enough synagogues, this *mitsvah* is permissible but not obligatory. Our rabbis also taught us that the world survives only because of the breath of schoolchildren [Shabbat 119b]; that no scholar should live in a city that lacks a primary teacher [Sanhedrin

17b]; that a father should teach his son the *Sh'ma* [Deuteronomy 6:4] as soon as he knows how to speak [Tosefta Chagigah 1:2]; that he who teaches his son Torah is merited as if he himself received it from Sinai [Kidushin 30a] . . . and many other sayings which cannot be spelled out here. We have displayed a brief selection of their words to show how greatly beloved the *mitsvah* of teaching Torah is in God's eyes (so great is it, that God himself yielded his honor before that of the Torah [Yerushalmi Chagigah, ch. 1:1]), and how much it is praised by our rabbis of blessed memory. If they said this in their generation of knowledge and learning—when biblical wisdom stood at its summit and the holy Talmud flowered like a daffodil in God's vineyard, when true purity and asceticism still existed, modesty and fear of sin had not ceased, men of action had not grown exhausted, and hoodlums had not grown mighty— then what can we possibly say? If in their day—with a generation that produced holy, pious scholars and scribes, rabbis, and teachers who taught wisely, judges who judged justly, and leaders who governed intelligently—they said that Joshua ben Gamla [who ordered primary schools established in every city, Baba Batra 21a] should be remembered gratefully, as without him Torah would have been forgotten in Israel— then what are we to do in our generation? In our generation almost all are guilty. Torah may, heaven forbid, vanish from Israel. Our Jewish brethren in the diaspora are in trouble, their minds daily thrown into turmoil by distresses and troubles thrust upon them by strong tormentors. Particularly in this land of freedom, the Torah rests in a corner gathering dust; her children do not seek out her greatness.

Knowing all this, can you keep silent in this hour of trouble, not doing a thing to uphold the holy Torah? If so, who knows what the end will be? Brethren, do not forget: if there are no students there can be no teachers. While the younger generation are still in their parental home, acting according to the laws of our holy religion, they still at times feel constrained to copy their parents, much as a monkey mimics a man. But who knows what the future will bring? Will they remain strong and interested after they cut their ties to their parental home? There is but one path ahead of us: to follow in the footsteps of Rabbi Joshua ben Gamla and establish everywhere primary teachers for our nation's poor. This must particularly be done in New York where our obligation is all the greater; the poor of one's own city [take precedence over those of another]. If we do this, then hope remains that Torah will not be, heaven forbid, forgotten by the poor of our nation in America (from whom will come forth Torah). The multitude of the righteous will be as shining stars forever. *Amen Selah.*

We hold high hopes that our call will not be lost in the desert, but having come deeply from within our hearts will enter straight into the hearts of our ever merciful Jewish brethren. May they heed our request as soon as possible by hurrying to participate in our great project, from which all Israel will derive benefits. Only then will our charitable work be completed.

We close with words of thanks and blessing to our friend, the distinguished author, both for his valuable book, written with good taste and wisdom, and filled with grace and charm, and for his goodhearted spirit of generosity in devoting all the proceeds of his work to the benefit of our needy society. We hope that all our generous countrymen, particularly those who love the beautiful rhythms of our holy tongue, will purchase this book either at its price or at any price that their generosity allows. And on this account, may the Holy One blessed be He protect and deliver them from all distress and illness, and bless all their efforts with success, along with all Israel their brethren. Amen—may it so be His will.

New York, Tuesday the 15th of Sivan 5647 [May 26, 1887]
The Directors of the Society

1 Synagogues

I will restore your magistrates as of old, and your counselors as of yore. After that you shall be called City of Righteousness, City of Faith (Isaiah 1:26).

It is impossible to know with precision how many Jews are living in New York, but according to estimates their number exceeds 100,000 or 120,000 families.[4] Most of them are resident aliens and immigrants: a few have come only to make money, with the thought later of returning; the majority have come to settle. They live here a life of freedom and liberty, and they enjoy, along with every citizen, full rights.

As in all large Jewish cities, so too here in New York, Jews are divided into many sects and parties; their rituals span the spectrum from one end to the other. New York Jews also belong to several new sects, the likes of which Europeans cannot imagine, they being without parallel in any of the cities and states of our native lands. But about these new sects in Israel, our writers have already written enough; there is practically nothing new to say. We shall in this volume, therefore, deal basically with the concerns of Orthodox Jews, believers in the faith. We shall speak about other parties only occasionally, here and there as the subject demands.

According to some people, the number of Orthodox congregations [in New York] totals 130; others bring the figure up to 240. Both are correct: the number of organized and settled congregations do indeed amount to 130; those who talk of a larger sum obviously include in their calculations small *minyanim*—those held in private homes and houses of study. Were they also to search in lofts and courtyards they might well even find many others, perhaps a total of as many as 300 or more.

Besides their congregations, our Orthodox brethren have many different associations and societies dedicated to acts of charity and righteousness. But these have nothing whatsoever to do with matters of faith and religion. We shall talk about them, God willing, in a separate section [see below, chapter 9].

The purposes and aims of most Orthodox congregations are to meet twice daily or every Sabbath for group worship; to visit and succor their sick; to bury and give last rites to their dead; and to extend financial aid in an hour of distress to loyal members.

But their more exalted aim is to build beautifully adorned synagogues. Every congregation that succeeds in doing this is boundlessly happy. Its members think that in this way they have fulfilled their every duty to Judaism.

The synagogues of our Orthodox brethren follow the Torah and its commandments and do not differ in any way from those of their fellow God-fearing Jews wherever they might live. The few of them that have slightly altered the place of the *bimah* [platform], the vestments of the reader, and so on are exceptions. These congregations were doubtless established many years ago, before the great rabbis of our generation pointed out how serious these things were; or in some cases they acted innocently, without realizing the implications of what they were doing.

Many congregations have, alongside their synagogue, another structure in which there is a special room called a *bes hamidrash* [house of study], so called because of the collection of books housed there in a closed cabinet. Occasionally this is opened by a few old men, the only remaining vestiges of the past, who learn—so to speak on one foot—a chapter of Mishnah or a page of Gemara. A poor visitor, not yet enlightened as to the ways of New York, might also come and take up a volume, perhaps to satisfy a natural inner urge; perhaps merely to escape from his sorrows.

In some congregations, the synagogue and the *bes hamidrash* are one. After the services five or six men stay behind to study the books. In a few, people regularly study Talmud together in groups. But these sessions don't generally last longer than half an hour, and are without depth and penetration. They are marked by confusion, anxiety, and haste, for most of the students are poverty-stricken men who must run out to find sustenance for their families.

The leaders, rulers, and administrators of a congregation are the *parnas* [president], his assistant, the treasurer, the secretary, and in some cases also the sexton. They stand at the helm; all is decided by their words. At congregational gatherings in the meetinghouse, people bring before their ruling throne all quarrels and contentions, every difficulty regardless of whether it falls under civil or criminal law. Along with other men selected by the congregation, they then render verdict, arrange for compromise, make peace between the warring parties, or bring the matter before a *din Torah* [litigation before a rabbinical court] whose word brooks no appeal.

In this great city of 100,000 Jews and 130 Orthodox congregations there are no more than three or four superior court rabbis, rabbis who decide what is prohibited and permitted. Even they were not called to assume these honorable posts. They rather came here, like everyone else, to find food, and located these positions only after a great deal of trouble and effort. Nor for a moment are they pleased with them, for their communities do not provide enough for their satisfaction. Indeed their regular salaries are so small that it would be shameful to record the amount in print. They thus live penuriously; a small communal stipend, combined with a few isolated gifts, barely cover their basic human needs.

Musar magidim [preachers of ethics], *ba'ale agadah* [experts on lore], and *darshanim* [expositors of Scripture] are found here by the hundreds, but only a very few of them succeed in acquiring positions. Necessity forces them to peddle their speeches from city to city, and from group to group; they are wanderers all of their days. *Darshanim* and *magidim* that are hired exclusively by congregations are treated just as poorly, and also have trouble surviving. To provide for themselves and their families they must engage in thousands of outside activites.

European communites considered officeholders and functionaries of the above-mentioned sort to be absolutely essential. So they scraped together their last monies to support both them and their students. But here they are considered to be old fashioned, outmoded antiques. Our brethren here know of the essential roles they have until now played in those Old World lands where Jews—still ignorant of the world's ways—continue to believe, as the rabbis put it, that the world cannot exist without Torah. They also know about the tanners [see Talmud Baba Batra 25a] who curbed their own expenses in order to support rabbis, preachers, and students, hoping to merit eternal reward and ultimate renewal through them. But the modern tanners, the unworthy generation that has merited to bask in the light of America, prefer a sweet-singing *chazan* [cantor] to all the rabbis, judges, preachers, and expositors in the world. They prefer one hour of contentment in the community hall to all the joy, satisfaction, and spiritual pleasure that their fathers found in studying the Torah, Prophets, and commentaries all together.

How are the terms "sweet-singing *chazan*" and "one hour of contentment in the synagogue" defined in America? In order for you to understand this, honored reader, I must first introduce you to several of the differences between synagogues here and in our native lands:

1. In all other lands congregants are unequal and treated accordingly, each man attaining honors commensurate with his status and worth. In America all are equal and treated alike. There is a dear and wonderful expression for this among the congregations here: "Equal hats make men equal."

2. In all other lands a man is required by the government to belong to the *kehilah* [community] of the area where he lives, and like it or not it levies taxes upon him. In America any may cut himself off from his community, taking no part in it whatsoever. One who remains loyal to his community and faith is deemed meritorious.

3. In all other lands the congregation gathers but once every three months, and even then only the leaders and overseers generally meet. In America the entire congregation gathers twice a month, or even once a week, not to speak of private meetings, which take place at any time.

4. In all other lands, a congregation appoints a *parnas* only once in three years, and it takes meticulous care not to appoint a man possessed of an unscrupulous past. In America the laws relating to the *parnas* are studied and expounded thirty days prior to each holiday [i.e., elections are held in spring and fall], and nobody is scrupulous about anything.

5. In all other lands, every city of at least 150 Jews appoints three judges, after carefully inspecting to make sure that they are men of great wisdom and discernment in the ways of the Torah: men of vast knowledge who at the same time are modest, upright, frugal, truthful, and lovers of humanity. In America one relies for everything on three laymen. They are found by inspecting everyone who displays haughtiness and greed, talks big, leaps forward to barge into other peoples' conversations, has a tall and handsome appearance, and cannot speak gently to his fellow human beings. First, such a one is made a trustee, then a treasurer, then a secretary, then a judge of minor matters, and from there he is raised to [the highest religious court], the *Bes Din Hagadol*. He is placed at the head of the community, given a golden scepter, which in this country is in the shape of a mallet, and with it he rules his people; he is at once their ruler and judge.

The consequences that result from these vigorous changes are numerous and vast, but here we shall consider only those that pertain to our subject. They are:

1. Many among the masses who, [isolated] in their native lands

never had many dealings with other people, have found friends here, and become more refined.

2. The less consequential members of our people, who never previously held opinions of their own, and who prior to their emigration had always been forced to answer an "amen" of assent to every idea that other people had put into their heads, have here earned the right to express their opinions publicly. They no longer have to depend on any counsel or opinion save their own. In a year or two, if fortune smiles upon them, they can even become prime movers. Then hundreds will eagerly anticipate their advice, and every word that comes out of their mouths will be savored.

3. Brazen outlaws, people who in their homeland were excluded from society, forced always to stand by the road asking passersby what was going on behind the closed doors of the town hall, hold their heads high in this country. They are like a cancer of thorns and thistles spreading amidst people of wisdom and ideas—never lacking, thank God, in any congregation—preventing them from boosting the community's honor and, consequently, that of Torah and Judaism.

4. And now the most remarkable consquence of all. The best of our people, who in their homelands went to the *bes midrash* to hear classes and pass their spare time, as well, on the other hand, as the most rotten who used to gather in the pubs and banquet halls to while away their time, find that all such things are unnecessary here. Both those who traditionally sat idle and those who traditionally sat learning run to the congregational meeting and find just what they have been seeking: merry fellowship. Night turns into day with them as they debate, split hairs, argue, and battle, make peace and compromise, all the while enjoying themselves immensely.

Those who seek Torah still have a large and honorable task ahead of them: the task that generally comes up after all immediate matters are taken care of. At this point the community's eloquent and knowledge-able men begin to inquire into matters of true value and benefit to the group, and we frequently hear words of Torah expounded according to their "plain" meaning. Should, for example, the society be named *Degel Machane Dan* [The Standard of the Division of Dan]? One expositor will brilliantly show how it was foretold from on high that someday a Jewish benefit society would carry that very name, and that Dan, who heads the society now named after him, would surely "govern his people and shepherd his flock as one of the tribes of Israel"—just as foreordained [cf. Genesis 49:16].

We hear at these meetings not just this form of Torah, but occasionally even penetrating sermons filled with a combination of Torah, wisdom, and practical knowledge. Remarkably, these meetinghouse orators always know how to illustrate their words with tales of their trials and tribulations—those encountered during their many long days at the machine shop and factory. And lo our meek brothers—newcomers to these shores who have just recently joined the community—at first sit fearfully as if among scorpions, filled with wonder at what they see: tailors, shoemakers, and tanners standing tall and expounding Torah to the multitude. In all their lives their eyes have never witnessed such things. They are used to hearing Torah from the mouths of rabbis, judges, and the like, people whose whole work is Torah. Here they see a whole new world before them—and more. For while these people lift up their heads, screaming ever louder on all manner of subjects, they espy those known to possess Torah and learning sitting on the side, hiding in the corner. No matter what the subject of discussion they always wind up on the losing end.

As the days proceed, the newcomers will relax. This is America, after all, and in America nothing is impossible. Just as America could invent the telephone, and transform many another wonder into a commonplace, so it can surely change the spirit of man by making the fools wiser, and the wise more foolish. That's what is meant by the phrase "equal hats make men equal."

Now, dear reader, you should be able to understand, if you have any feelings at all, how much satisfaction and benefit these tanners receive from their current situation. You should be able to tell your friends in Russia, Poland, and Hungary what one hour of pleasure in an American community hall really is, and how it should be valued. I deeply regret not being able to tell you more things, to give you a total picture of the communal gatherings here. But if I told you everything, I would be unable to exclude merriment and jokes. And while the heart within me rages and my soul feels degraded, I abstain from merrymaking. Sighs and bitter tears are more appropriate here.

2 "Kosher" Meat

Shochatim [ritual slaughterers] and butchers, upon whose shoulders rest all responsibility for the laws of *kashrus* and *tarfus* [they decide what is kosher and what is not], are perfectly independent here; neither they nor their work is inspected. Congregations do not hire their own *shochatim*—either they don't want to or don't have the means—and the work of *shechitah* [ritual slaughtering] here is thus like all other jobs: it can be undertaken by anyone who finds an opening. Indeed, the situation is actually worse in this case, for in all other lines of work at least the factory bosses know whom to hire, whom to advance, and whom to fire. The slaughterhouse bosses do not know how to discern good from bad, since most are not Jewish, or are American-born Jews who know as little about Judaism as the reader knows about mountaintops—and could care less. The upshot is that in our slaughterhouses each man takes what he can get: the one who knows how to plume his own feathers, take pride in his own righteousness and virtue, shrivel up and disappear in time of crisis, act hypocritically and inconsistently, tongue-lash his fellows, and convince himself that none is like unto him—he will be the "holy one," and unto him all Israel will sacrifice both money and soul.

We cannot hide the fact that in our community there are, thank God, also outstanding *shochatim,* wonderful specialists who work both rapidly and expertly. They have certificates from leading Jews in Europe attesting to their skills, their good conduct, and their piety. These *shochatim* have already striven mightily to bring about improvements. Last year [1885] they joined together into a dear and honorable organization named the *Zivchei Tomim* Society, and several rabbis here took it upon

46

themselves to give them and their customers ritual supervision (*hash-gachah*) with the hope of "straightening the crooked" and removing all obstacles. But no sooner did we happily tell ourselves that "we are saved; from now on even the poor can eat and be satisfied," than this organization went the way of every good and useful thing in America. It lasted no longer than [Jonah's] gourd, coming one night, dying the next. Now, instead of seeing improvements, we find that new unforeseen difficulties have arisen. Not a day goes by without screams and quarrels between *shochatim* and butchers. Each side composes and spreads libelous documents about the other, stinging and battling, while Israel looks on, its sight failing, helpless.

We have a large number of poultry *shochatim* here. While it was still legal for merchants to keep live birds in their shops, anyone could come, take his live goose or chicken, and bring it to the *shochet* of his choice. But since the [city] government ordained that it was henceforth illegal to keep live fowl for sale in the stores, and that all poultry should be slaughtered in a specific spot outside the city, a whole host of new troubles have arisen in New York. We now face a whole series of terrible obstacles, quite apart from the noise, the bustle, the fighting, the shame, indeed, the desecration of God's very name that we always see in this foul valley [Gouverneur Slip?], which has assumed the appearance of hell.

The four primary causes of injury are as follows:

1. The location. It is excessively narrow, and forever filled with rivers of mud, mire, and blood. Throngs of frightened, impetuous people stand crowded together, each one pushing the other. The *shochatim* must stand as if encaged. They lack room to turn left or right, and even the ability to move their hands.

2. The time. Since most of the fowl is slaughtered on Sabbath eve, or on Thursday, every slaughterhouse boss understandably wants to get a head start, for the earlier he gets to market, the greater his success. The *shochet,* therefore, must sometimes slay as many as 200 birds, or more, in one breath. Woe to the pious and God-fearing, but the commands of the boss standing over him take precedence, and do not permit even a moment's rest. So the *shochet*, though his soul troubles him, continues so long as he has strength within him. His Maker understands his plight.

The *shochet* knows that he did not properly sharpen the knife or inspect it more than once, and even then in a great hurry. He knows that he made mistakes, and slaughtered some [fowl] improperly. But what can the wretchedly poor *shochet* do? He has to maintain his wife and children and this is his main source of support. So he lifts up his soul to

God, and, given no choice, recalls to himself the words of the rabbis: poverty diverts man from the knowledge of his Creator; penitence restores him [Eruvin 41b].

3. The salesmen-butchers. Many of them are not of the highest caliber. As far as they are concerned, any slaughtered fowl with blood removed is marketable, even if the *shochet* admits that he slaughtered totally impermissibly both by missing the mark and by cutting under cover, or even that he never completed the slaughter at all, but that the overseer, observing that the bird was about to die, sliced through its neck. This nevertheless is insufficient to disqualify the fowl, according to the "reliable" and "honest" butcher, who keeps his store shuttered on the Sabbath. But though he does no work, he is not nearly as scrupulous about resting his animal, which he takes to the marketplace, so he can buy his provisions. Of course, he does so "only for the sake of the poor," in order that everything might be ready for them on Sunday, including a fat chicken. He knows his customers are not among the scrupulous, and could not care less whether the slaughter took place from the front of the neck or from the back of it. Even those who are scrupulous cannot understand these matters. And if faced with an occasional wise customer who does understand, the butcher places all guilt on the head of the *shochet*—who is made to pay for the sin.

4. The *shochatim* themselves. They are the main cause, for however much one may vindicate them and blame the butchers, there remains the question of why their blood is redder than anybody else's [i.e., why should they be allowed to cause somebody else's sin?] We return therefore to the law of "each man takes what he can get," the procedure long followed in the large animal slaughtering houses. They have problems of their own, as we have already mentioned, but they are not of the same scope and magnitude as the obstacles and corruptions found in this terrible place. At least in the large abattoirs each *shochet* is his own master with a room of his own. Here absolute anarchy reigns, and all—no matter how great their number—dwell together in the same cage. There the long-recognized expert *shochatim* and the unrecognized much-complained-about *shochatim* have both served abroad under rabbis and teachers for many years. They conduct themselves properly in this country as well, and nothing personally ugly is heard about them, except what one says about the other, as is normal in all lines of work.

The situation is quite different here. My pen almost refuses to describe things as they truly are—loathesome and disgraceful. Perhaps it is best to be silent; all who want to know the truth should visit the place to see with their own eyes. Let our words not cause further desecration of God's name, especially since we cannot improve matters. We add only this: to our great sorrow we sometimes see *shochatim* who look as though they had learned their art hurriedly, while standing on one foot, a month before they left their native lands. Then there are those who served in this profession when they first started out in life, but were corrupted and removed from office by the rabbis. Now they have come here to try their hand again. Finally there are those who never in their lives dreamed of being ritual slaughterers, but after years of business, trade, and other kinds of swindling, became poultry slaughterers overnight. And the masses of God's people, among them the righteous and pure, follow these men and eat of their meat; they know not how they stumble.

Those who sell Jews meat are also fully independent here, and with the exception of a few who are under supervision, they all live in a world of lawlessness. Nobody oversees them or pays attention to their deeds. Every tongue and pen should publicize the problems connected with this situation. There are those who are not embarrassed to take improperly slaughtered meat and to sell it publicly to innocent people, notwithstanding the fact that their stores are anointed in huge gilded letters with the words KOSHER MEAT. Then there are those who are clever enough to satisfy all sides with their actions. They take their meat from the kosher slaughterhouse, complete with six seals of supervision. But everything else—like the spleen, the heart, the liver, and similar parts that American women crave—these they buy from anyone, even from abattoir sales of improperly slaughtered and otherwise nonkosher meat. Thus they increase their business and attract customers, for a Jewish woman here, even a modest one, is more likely to search after places that sell the above-mentioned parts in large numbers than she is to seek a reliable, God-fearing butcher. A pile of bones and a large piece of spleen are more important to her than the *kashrus* of the butcher and the meat in his store put together.

The masses err in that they never heard, even in their native lands, of rabbis meticulously scrutinizing sellers of meat, or taking the trouble to appoint butchers who are wise and God-fearing. To the contrary, they have always considered the butchers to be ignorant and simpleminded; even the best among them being known as "partners of Amalek" [Kidushin 82a]. But nobody ever charged the butchers with subverting [*kashrus*]! Therefore, when the "greener" [the new immigrant] comes here and is told by his acquaintances that the meat dealer in their neighborhood does not buy his goods from the general marketplace, it never occurs to him to investigate further. Knowing that the butcher is neither a rabbi nor a *shochet,* he assumes that no attention need be paid to his moral quality. His eyes merely see the large seal [of *kashrus*] hanging over the meat in the windows of his shop. He does not realize how different the situation is from that which existed in his old small town where the *shochet* knew exactly how many animals he slaughtered, and how many of them were kosher and non-kosher. Nor even was this really necessary, for in our small towns every stone had seven eyes! People knew everything that was done and said, even behind closed doors. Not even the stupidest butcher or a non-Jew could make any problems—which is not true here, where even if all the *shochatim* joined together to monitor a particular butcher, he could still mislead them. Who could force him to show what was out back in the icehouse? Who could inspect what was hidden in holes and crevices—bones, thighs, hoofs, stomachs, intestines, several types of livers, and lungs? Such are the parts that women desire prepared: sprinkled with purifying waters, changed, and sprinkled again [i.e., salted and soaked in the prescribed manner]. But this is not done to soften the meat or to remove from it existing blood; not to observe, heaven forbid, the commandments of the rabbis and *poskim.* It is done only to remove the dirt and stench, for the majority of improperly slaughtered, unkosher meat that is sold here in the market is meat that has lain around for more than three days. The butcher must take constant and scrupulous care to see that it does not begin to reek. So great is the scandal in this great holy city, that thousands of honest families who fear and tremble at the thought of their straying into one tiny prohibition or sin never realize or suspect that they are eating all sorts of unkosher meat, carcasses trodden underfoot. Indeed they utter blessings over the meat before partaking of it, and pronounce grace when they are done. No one takes it upon himself to warn them, for in our day the wise keep silent. He who has the temerity to open his mouth in public is told to take his good advice and junk it.

3 Education

There is nothing in the way of schooling here for the young men of Israel. Our faithful Orthodox brethren, who pride themselves on not seeking reforms, and revel in their own piety and righteousness, unhesitatingly allow their sons to grow up without Torah or faith. They don't mind that their children, while still babes, run after lucre, a life of pleasure, and all human gratifications—forgetting altogether their faith, Torah, and holy roots. Instead of training their sons to follow in their ways, they spend their time inspecting cantors, *parnasim*, sextons, and other synagogue officials. They heed not the march of time as it rages, billows, and slowly destroys the best part of Jewry.

Chadarim [religious elementary schools] where teachers [*melamdim*] give instruction in the alphabet, vowels, and Hebrew reading are found here in abundance; such abundance, in fact, that their fees have fallen tremendously. According to reports, many teachers have now issued a handbill in which they agree to teach any Jewish child, however he may be—rich or poor, bright or dumb—for only ten cents a week, or forty cents a month. Obstinate householders won't take advantage of this bargain. They tell themselves that just as the price has fallen, so it will fall again—until teachers uncomplainingly accept fees of a mil an hour. But they are wrong on two counts: (1) until this happens their sons will forget everything they ever knew, forcing their parents to start paying all over again from the beginning; (2) what they foresee will never happen. We have already heard teachers whispering that if they do not win their battle, and cannot improve their lot, they will abandon teaching completely and return to sewing clothes, tanning leather, or making shoes— each to the job that he performed in his native land.

More advanced teachers [*morim*] with wisdom and learning are also found here in abundance, and many of them are wonderfully skillful, highly trained pedagogues. But in the absence of schools, and in the absence of any desire on the part of many of our brethren to rear their sons on "the knees" of Torah, they have trouble finding steady work. After a few years of shuffling about as if in a world of desolation, most of them give up and return shamefacedly to their homelands. The lucky ones, who successfully make their way after a great deal of grief and travail into the homes of our wealthier brethren and are handed their sons, find it impossible to use their knowledge. They must rather wrack their brains to recall what they studied in their childhood from primary teachers. For during the period when, in our native lands, they taught Jewish children Torah from beginning to end, they must teach the sagacious children here the Hebrew alphabet, from *alef* to *tov*. And during the time when the Hungarian or Polish Jewish youngster was brought to a level where he could understand the Prophets, and listen to rigorous biblical and legal studies, the American youngster is merely brought to the magnificent level of being able to stammer a few words of English-style Hebrew, to pronounce the blessing over the Torah, and to chant half the *maftir* [the weekly prophetic portion] from a text with vowels and notes on the day he turns thirteen—a day that is celebrated here as the greatest of holidays among our Jewish brethren. From that day onward a youngster considers his teacher to be an unwanted article. On the very day of the celebration— the day when his father stops assuming responsibility for his sins—an angel comes, slaps him on the mouth, and [just as happens, according to legend, at birth] he forgets all the Torah that he has learned, including the blessings, the *maftir,* and, of course, the phylacteries. In their place he must learn to establish for himself a goal in life, and to become familiar with the ways of the world. The teacher is thus unnecessary. And since the parents come from Poland, and "know" that this wisdom does not require the service of a trained and learned pedagogue, they have no use for the teacher, no matter what his quality. They pay, therefore, only according to their own estimate of what his work is worth—an amount generally so small that one cannot possibly live on it. Teaching has thus become a scorned and debased profession. It does not support those engaged in it, and none will choose it save a man who, having tried his hand at all else, finally senses that his lucky star has gone black and that he is fated to see only dark days for all the rest of his life.

Among our Orthodox brethren here there are two Talmud Torah

schools for children of the poor. One of them is already in ruins, its staff about to collapse from lack of support. The second [Machzike Talmud Thora], thank God, still stands strong on number 83 East Broadway.[5] Some 400 students study there. This house of study was set up four years ago [1883] through the efforts of important and honorable men—lovers of their people and religion—whose spirits never darkened, no matter how hard they toiled. They let money flow from their own pockets, knocked on the doors of large donors, and occasionally even aroused the leaders of our brethren, asking them for a hand in aid of their project. Finally they succeeded in setting up the house that now stands in full majestic splendor: a miracle, a true wonder. The teachers, all men of wisdom and learning, perform their work with perfect integrity. The founders, now as in the past, never tire of doing all in their power to increase the honor and glory of their institution. According to the testimony of many who understand the field of education, this school can compete successfully with any school of its kind in our native lands.

Would that there were many in this city like the founders and leaders of this school, men of Torah, piety, charity, righteousness, and virtue. Would that many would examine and reflect on their laudable actions, on the goodness and righteousness that they are performing for the sake of their people and faith. Let them support this work with their right hands—their money, their strength, their every endeavor—so that this school can truly become an honored and praised place in this city and country. I, the writer, am filled with feelings of gratitude toward the founders, leaders, directors, teachers, and overseers of this school, all men of good heart, excellent spirit, and God-fearing piety.

As a sign of my gratitude, I shall, God willing, write a special article to describe this first school of its kind in the history of Orthodox Judaism in America: its activities until now, its hopes for the future, the confidence of its teachers, its remarkable educational success in teaching our Torah and faith, and the virtues of its founders and supervisors who provide the students with spiritual and material sustenance, as well as shelter. Like good fathers, they sacrifice all their strength for the sake of these "poor lambs"; without them, the children would wander the main roads, like so many other wild urchins of their age in this city do, much to the regret of everyone who loves his people and religion. What an invaluable project! Praise to all concerned with it! May God remember them fondly!

Still there are two things that must be complained about: (1) Since our brethren have seen that even in New York it is possible for students to excel in the study of Hebrew, religion, and our holy Torah, why don't they—its supporters—send their own children to the school? These honorable men have fulfilled the rabbinic dictum, "Be mindful of the children of the poor, for from them will come forth Torah" [Nedarim 81a]. Why do they not also fufill the Torah's command to "teach your children" [Deuteronomy 11:19]? (2) The school's directors, in spite of all their work and effort, have not succeeded in setting up divisions for the teaching of Mishnah and Talmud in the manner we are accustomed to in our native lands.

Supporters of the school are still too few in number. We know that many of our brethren, even those who are close to the school and well aware of its virtues, have not yet donated a penny to aid its great and holy work upon which rests all our hopes for the future. It is, however, nothing for them to donate on just one occasion, when they are called to the Torah, $20 or more for the support of the *chazan* and the choir. Oh when will our brethren understand? When will they finally see the light?

Uptown our Orthodox brethren have another two or three schools for beginners. But the number of students who take instruction there are few, since congregations established these for their own members; an outsider may not attend.

The most respected of these schools stands on 57th Street and belongs to the magnificent and renowned congregation known as Adath Israel, or the 57th Street Schule. One of the teachers in this school is an excellent and wise man, of great learning and tremendous piety; one of the few members of the uptown elite in the whole city. Not only the youths given over to him for guidance in the foundations of Torah and piety benefit from his wisdom and advice, but also their parents, honorable members of the congregation. They now delight in his Torah and wisdom, and treat him with enormous respect.

It has already occurred to the leaders of the community to place this man in a rabbinical position so that he might receive the glory that he deserves. But for reasons that we do not know, this dear man does not want to accept so honorable a post. Even without it he maintains himself with dignity, sits in a tent of Torah and wisdom, and is beloved of all who know and respect his superior merit.

The teacher who preceded him in this school and served honorably for many years, was also a man of great spirit and enormous learning— an eminent, diligent, and wise old scholar, full of exalted virtues and great moral excellence. Three years have passed since he voluntarily left his position. Now he rests on the laurels of his honor and success.

We can judge the quality of the members of this community from the quality of its teachers. The community respects scholars and honors Divine teaching. God be with it! May its members and their children be honored! May all who see them recognize that they are a people whom the Lord has blessed.

The noted and respected Hebrew Free School, where about 2,500 poor students receive instruction in Hebrew Bible reading, the basic fundamentals of Judaism, and the story of Israel's development, brought a great deal of good into the Jewish world of this city. Many, many Jewish poor here would, at age twenty, be unable to read a single letter from the prayerbook had not the gates of this school been opened to them in their youth, totally without cost. Unfortunately our own pious brethren do not participate in this valuable work. It depends, rather, on the contributions of the rich: from wealthy members of the new moderate factions and from a few Orthodox Jews of German and Dutch descent.

Just as we were concluding our words on teachers and schools, we heard the pleasant news that, in recent days, a new school was established here called *Yeshivas Ets Chayim*[6] [Tree of Life Yeshiva] for the study of Mishnah and Talmud, that is, Gemara, Rashi, and Tosafos. Fifteen hundred people are supposed to be standing ready to finance the building and appoint eminent teachers who will receive their salaries in honorable fashion from a large community fund. All is said to be prepared, nothing is lacking save for people willing to hand their children over for instruction. Hurrah! What pleasant news! How lovely! How dear! A yeshiva for Mishnah and Gemara! How much good is hidden in these words. I can hardly believe my own ears. Am I awake! Is this possible? Can it be? Here in New York? In America? Has such a great thing come about without our knowledge? Yes—so many people say, and so we have seen ourselves in news reports. It is a marvelous thing—a wonder.

We, who have heard nothing about this subject until now, can say only this: we yearn with all our heart to see that these reports are true and accurate, and that such a school has indeed been established. Now if only we can also see that it was not established on a false foundation, fleetingly, for a day or a month; that it was not established merely to increase the number of our *parnasim* and communal leaders, or to add to the amount of jealousy, hatred, and disagreement among us; and that it was not established to compete with the school that has already won a name for itself, lest both of them fail. Instead, may it have been established for the sake of God and His teachings: to ascertain truth, to spread Torah in Israel, and to strengthen the faith. If so, then without hesitation all who cling to the Lord and fear Him will, even without being asked, come to participate in this good work. Those worthies who assist that fine organization, the Machzike Talmud Thora, will also not withhold their support, but will perhaps try to give them as much or more. For these brethren know—or should know—that even if they succeed after a long, long time in enabling all our American boys to understand the Bible, know Hebrew, and investigate Jewish history, American Judaism will still lack a proper supporting foundation so long as it is without the essential ingredient: Talmud, the living, animating spirit behind our ancient nation; Israel's soul, spirit, strength, and valor all rolled into one. So let us reiterate our words: if what we have heard is true, if such a school has been established in Israel, if such valuable souls are indeed found in New York, then we shall come and extend to them our best. We shall unite and join with them, to help them increase the honor of this school until it stands as a tall fortress, exalting the majesty of Israel throughout this country.

4 Work

Those expertly learned in the Torah, the Talmud, and the wisdom of our blessed rabbis are, thank God, numerous in this city. Some of them settled in this land years ago and have been blessed by God with wealth, honor, and property. We cannot say, however, that they have succeeded in at once sitting at two tables: that of Torah and that of wealth. They, rather, prefer their money, and to that they devote all their attention. They do not set aside special times for Torah, and do not attend classes. All they know is what they learned as children. The bulk of the learned, however, are wretchedly poor immigrants who have come here only in the last few years. They have abandoned their Torah only from necessity—much against their will. They spend all their time toiling. The only joy they have in this world is when they find a place to revive.

The occupations of these impoverished ones are well known: tailoring, sewing, and ironing—all in the garment trade; portering; pack-carrying; peddling; and begging. These are all delightful and magnificent occupations for pampered men, filled to the brim with pearls of Torah, who never in their lives attempted to stick the tips of their fingers into water. But what else can these unfortunate refugees do? "Do whatever you can to survive," the Americans say, and their words are perfectly correct. For if they do not save themselves on the strength of their own blood, sweat, and tears, but rather rely on Torah and wisdom, then they'll be lost forever. So much of their time do these people spend on trying, contemptible, and burdensome labors, that all their days are used up. How can they spend money to coddle themselves, to enjoy the delights of mankind, when they return home in the evening or dead of night exhausted? All their lusts and cravings have left them; they are happy just to find a place to rest from toil, sadness, and rage. Their goal is not to gather wealth and become rich, or to save pennies until they can return and set down roots in some secure area of their homeland. The good days when one could do that have passed from the American scene. Now poverty, privation, and want are firmly ensconced here too. They rather work entirely in order to eat; daily bread is their reward and portion.

He whom God has not blessed with sons, daughters, and a large household where all can contribute by doing their own work; he who will not turn his small house into a boarding home for twenty workers and peddlers, subsisting on their leavings, and taking upon himself to sleep on the earth; he who cannot parade around in worn-out rags, and purchase patchwork garments in old-clothes stores; he who does not wish to encamp on the sixth floor, and to grovel before the landlord once a month to lower or forgive the rent; he who does not understand reality, does not know how to deceive, does not live in a world of hypocrisy, does not enjoy leading people astray, and does not consciously bait people by telling them lies—such a one will never see an extra cent in his purse. His means will remain ever the same.

We have not told you these things in order to describe the means of business and support employed by most of our brother immigrants. Our major aim in this book is rather devoted to delicate spiritual matters. We have no concern now with matters of material life, nor have we come, dear reader, in order to preach morality to you, to rouse you to the lot of these unfortunates, or to tell you to support them so that they might return to spending time on Torah and law. For we know that no sooner would our words enter your right ear than they would exit via your left. After all, the moral lessons of the rabbi's preaching don't even excite you—and he knows to marshal his words with taste and knowledge; knows to be careful not to treat you frivolously, or to affront, heaven forbid, your honor. How then should you come and listen to a moral reproof from the author! Truth be told, he does appear to love eternally his people and Torah. But there is no stopping the flow of his words! Coals glow when he talks. He shows no special favor to a man even if he towers as high as a cedar. He tells things as they are, without makeup or adornment. He displays truth as naked as the day it was born: something inconsistent with the spirit of the time and the place. American readers will not find him compelling.

Thus, not for you or for people like you have these words been written. We cast our sights to our brothers in the more remote diaspora, our honored readers in Russia, Poland, and Hungary. To you we have devoted this chapter: to the poor unfortunate man who in the midst of his sorrows may perhaps have considered coming here to seek a fortune. You have neither money nor tools, neither skills nor work. All you know is that you are a young scholar. So listen to us, and tough it out: stay home. No matter how many fine letters or documents are in your hands from brilliant rabbis who will recommend you and praise your skills highly, you will be unable to lead a rabbinical life. Teachers on various levels, and *shochatim*, are already found in abundance, and from what has already been said, you know how well they succeed. There are, to be sure, other sources of support for people like you, but we don't want to deal with them just yet. When you do come to that point in your reading which we have set aside for these subjects, you will see for yourself that they hold no promise of success either.

The only possible source of support is itinerant preaching, for it is not limited to any one place or community. In an emergency, you can move on and peddle your speeches from city to city. But even with luck, you won't draw much. The competition is great, consequently the job has fallen to the lowest level. A regular preacher's salary now amounts to only $200 at most. An occasional sermon brings no more than $2 or $3, and sometimes only $1.50. Generally this is collected on Sunday from congregational notables who rage and storm but usually give something rather than sending the preacher away empty-handed. Besides this— besides the competition, the fatigue, the scorn, and the toil—it is most difficult to please an American audience. If, dear sir, you know yourself not to be a man of parables, a man of vanity and conceit, a man with a treasure-trove of legends and stories, a man who punctuates his words with empty rhetoric and meaningless bombast, a man who can extract good from evil, a man who can weave his ideas around relevant events and live individuals, a man who knows how to exploit his Torah either by building himself up majestically and scorning all those who wish to speak with "his eminence" or by grinding himself down to the dust and fawningly acting as everyone's doormat, dancing to the tune of all whose favors and benefits he needs—if, my dear sir, you are not a man who can do all these things, then you will never succeed here as a preacher. Nothing will be left for you to do save dressing in black, wrapping your-self up in shrouds, and rolling from darkness to abyss: from factory, to sweatshop, to itinerant peddling. For such great successes you don't need

America! You don't need to endanger your life by crossing great stretches of water! There, in your homeland and your own little city, you can do just as well if you only work diligently and put all fears of shame behind you.

And so my faithful advice to you, dear brother, is to stand firm, and stay where you are. Don't wander away. If the impetuous ones entice and fill you with longing, pay them no heed. You are not as strong as they are, and your thoughts run along different lines. Put your trust in the Lord! He will support you where you are, in the place of your forefathers, your brothers, and your friends; in the place where support for the learned who sit and study Torah is not deemed sinful; in the place where study is considered a regularly necessary part of Orthodox Jewish life; and in the place where, if you improve and succeed in your studies, you may still hope to sit at the highest level, at the seat of the great in learning. Then will your name be known in Israel, and benefits will flow to you, your household, your children, and your children's children forever.

5 Hebrew Culture

Relative to the large Jewish population here, the number of Hebrew authors, poets, and intellectuals is very small (may God increase their numbers), and their lot is like that of most authors since the beginning of time. Some act as teachers at the primary or secondary level, some are assistants in business, some are workers and artisans, some are peddlers, some are merchants, and most are just plain poor. At times they may work four shifts in a row, until they themselves no longer know who they are, what they are doing, and what their mission is.

Hebrew authors here cannot make much use of their knowledge or skills, and only occasionally is something of theirs seen in a book or a journal. Why then are they called authors? Because while still in their homelands they embittered their lowly lives with literary activities. But since they came to America, their eyes have been opened. They have seen that intellectual endeavors are futile. Futile too is the endeavor to preserve the outposts of knowledge, for no one will ever in this way be able to produce enough food for his body to maintain himself. So they have turned their backs and chosen to address other subjects. Instead of soaring high on the wings of poetry and song, or burrowing deeply into the world of culture, investigating and enriching scholarship, language, and literature, they delve relentlessly into the practical world, the world of the present. They concern themselves with affairs of the stomach: with livelihood and similar subjects relevant to the nitty-gritty of existence. They sink up to their necks in a torrent of present-day banalities and material possessions, just like all the rest of their Jewish brethren in this city and land.

Despite the dearth of skillful authors, we do have here a great number of Hebrew readers. Hebrew-language European periodicals and all the books, new ones and old ones, produced by our nation's skilled literary figures are read in many Jewish homes here omnivorously, in delight and love. Readers include excellent, virtuous, and valuable men, wealthy and honorable persons of eminence, who bask in the reflected light of scholars, and support them generously and magnanimously. But alas their numbers are few; even a child can count them. Most of our Hebrew readers, much as they love the language and the books written in it, neither respect its authors nor honor and support them (see Author's Note A). Their reasons and explanations are understandable: an author is no more similar to a book than a cause to an effect. [As Samson's riddle reminds us,] out of the strong can come something sweet [see Judges 14:14].

A key principle among Jews holds that authors do not touch their own books, not even by a hair's-breadth. Some like no books at all. But that lasts only so long as none comes their way. If by chance a volume does come into their hands, or if they see one by a friend, then they read it joyfully. But to pay money for it, to expend a living American dollar for a dead book, that they cannot bring themselves to do. They think to themselves how foolish men are who scatter their money on flowery letters without realizing that even a little common sense is more precious than wisdom and honor, how much more so the mighty and lovely dollar that has a great deal of beauty, and some usefulness as well. It is clearly more valuable than wisdom, honor, and all Israel's ancient and modern literature combined.

6 Periodicals and Their Religious Views

We have about four or five Jewish periodicals written in English [*The American Hebrew, The Hebrew Journal, The Hebrew Leader, The Hebrew Standard,* and *The Jewish Messenger*]. All of them veil their beliefs, but are considered by our brethren to be mouthpieces of Conservative Judaism. A reader from the old generation won't find anything in the papers to prove this. Articles invariably deal with our enlightened co-religionists from all parties and groups. Issues are always filled with sermons, novellae, news about rabbis, stories, announcements, activities, events, and occurrences—items that disagree totally with the brand of Judaism that the journals profess.

One journal alone [*The Hebrew Standard*] stands out as different. It set itself to fight for true old-time Judaism, and it regularly backs up its words with notable articles, filled with love and respect for the Torah, which God wrote and handed down—articles that produce purity of faith and piety. To be sure, those who regularly read this journal will see that it does not always fulfill its object. Its words sometimes appear self-contradictory. On the one hand, it will extol age-old Judaism and portray in brilliant colors the many benefits that proceed from its hallowed customs and time-honored constraints. On the other hand, in the very same issue it will laud and acclaim the leading sectarians, people who lie almost totally "over the line" outside Judaism, and who distance themselves with all their might from the life of Torah, the highest form of religious life. Because of the names falsely assumed by these groups—Conservatives, Liberals, and the like—the editor [Jacob P. Solomon][7] favors them with a special section. Here he reverently recalls the deeds of the greats:

the strength and courage of the notables that Israel has always had in its midst. While marveling at their wisdom, Torah, righteousness, holiness, and dedication, he proceeds to praise the new preachers. He prints their philosophies, sermons, and speeches, and extols their merits with all sorts of praises, although they are in no sense comparable to those who earlier stirred his heart.

Still, this periodical stands shoulder to shoulder in the battle against radical Jews. To them it never shows favor. When it does talk about their innovations and tactics, it is only in order to heap abuse, to blacken their faces in disgrace. Its war with them is eternal: ever will it struggle and strive against their members, rabbis, and ways.

We will not presume to judge or reprove this wise editor, for we understand the nature of his readership. We realize that these days a periodical publisher must also serve as a dealer and salesman—just like everyone else. Much as one could not tell a storekeeper to fight with his customers, so one cannot tell an editor to attack his. Otherwise his buyers will go elsewhere. The honorable editor may understand this as well as I do. Perhaps he sees his own inconsistencies, but cannot prevent them. So he throws dust in the eyes of his readers, and employs hints where he could otherwise say nothing. To penetrate the inner meaning of his words, the intelligent reader must read between the lines. Of course there is also another possibility. Perhaps the honorable editor, who grew up in this country, sees and judges things from a different vantage point than we who were educated the old way. Whatever the case, our aim is not to criticize his words. The honorable editor's value remains undiminished in our eyes, notwithstanding such sins as we have disclosed, which are hardly his alone these days. We merely wish to alert the reader to the confusion that reigns supreme here in all matters. Both among the observant Orthodox and among the enlightened innovators we find an abundance of "undecideds" who cannot be classified. It is impossible to know to which side they belong, or where to enter them. In general it is hard to find here anything—any subject whatsoever—where the purpose, goal, and principle are clear. In America the basis and root of all is the dollar: money answers everything. Just as money always revolves round and round, so too opinions and principles. Monetary considerations—value, expense, large or small profit, dollars! That's the principle. That's the goal. That's honor, strength, and the only reliably acceptable testimony. For most people in this city and nation, that is the single basis upon which all is evaluated.

Having touched on this subject, we cannot forbear giving you our own views. As we see it, dear readers, all the new parties have the same value; only two or three inches separate them. Ultimately they will all unite, for a single spirit binds them. We do not believe that American Judaism can hope for much, not from the radicals, the conservatives, the liberals, nor even from those who have just recently begun to alter their ways. Such is the nature of innovations these days: today it allows a man to do this, and tomorrow that. In the end he denies all, and makes of everything lofty, holy, and sublime one everlasting ruin.

He who recalls the history of societies and congregations here understands how much truth there is to our words. Who knows better than the editor mentioned above? He sees that almost all the innovative congregations, as well as those on the fringes, where there is not even a remnant of something holy, used to be considered God-fearing and pious. The great and venerable congregation B[eth El] that now stirs up heaven and earth with its plans for a beautiful temple to be erected with due magnificence in the heart of the city, and which has already succeeded, with the assent of the great lights in Cincinnati and New York, in promulgating every new reform and in mercilessly uprooting all memories of that which has been precious to Israel since ancient times—this congregation just thirty years ago was holy and faithful. In its day it stood first in importance. Its glory reflected on all other congregations in this city and state.

He knows that the large, wealthy congregation E[manu-El], known universally on account of the excellent preachers that it always imports from afar, has chopped down as with an ax everything that is holy to the Jewish people. Yet just twenty years ago it sparkled with faith and piety, and was considered among the leading congregations in New York. We have even heard it said that their former rabbi [Leo Merzbacher?[8]], later a leading Reformer, acted piously for years. In the first year of his arrival he belonged to the "morning dippers" [those who ritually immerse themselves in the *mikvah* every morning], and his congregants greatly revered him for it.

He knows, and so testified in his last issues, that many of the rabbis who have been trying for the last few years to uproot the whole basis of our religion were only a few years ago considered to be pious men, scrupulous observers of the commandments. Their congregations used to walk in God's path and observe the Torah.

Tell us, Mr. Editor, why did such transformations take place? Who or what caused the scandalous abominations that we now witness? Was it extensive, penetrating, and assiduous study of various sciences? Did they, heaven forbid, enter the *Pardes* [the garden of esoteric philosophy], look around, and sustain injury while investigating what is beyond both the natural order and the mind's grasp?

Actually anyone who follows the affairs and activities of our brethren here knows that their real knowledge and deepest concerns lie in wealth, comforts, and diversions. Nobody's faith here ever was weakened by scholarship and philosophy. He also knows that even rabbis who minister and pastor—with the exception of a few worthies who love learning and pursue it diligently—generally occupy their days with social gatherings, receptions, and benefits. In their free time they prettify their speech, trill their voices, and invent pleasant stories and homilies to pepper their lectures. That is the extent of their contribution to the world of learning, scholarship, and science. [Real] investigations are not injurious, and in themselves pose no risk. The most pious of preachers undertake them—and still remain unassimilated.

Who then is responsible for this perversity? Who brought down upon us this great [religious] destruction?

To be sure, reforms did not occur all at one time. Congregations did not suddenly turn about from one extreme to the other. Those faithful to Torah and religiosity did not overnight become utter and complete heretics. Our brethren, rather, began by opening to themselves the tiniest crevice, no wider than a needle. They aimed at first neither to uproot, to destroy, nor to remove, heaven forbid, even a single branch attached to the tree of Torah and religious essentials. They merely wanted to beautify Judaism's exterior, to adorn its head with a crown, to add to it beauty and grace, to modernize it, to make it compatible with life. They considered this first step to be a permissible, even a mandatory one because of the needs of the hour. They only dealt with insignificant matters, ones that came neither directly from Sinai nor from the early rabbinic masters of blessed memory. But this first step encouraged them to move forward; bit by bit they began to innovate and reform ever larger, more serious matters: the basic essentials. So weak did they become in their Torah, *mitsvos* [commandments] and deeds, that they eventually abandoned even those things that formed the foundation for the whole structure of Judaism.

What brought upon us this terrible upheaval were thus those changes and innovations that appear to be insignificant, what we would today consider to be small sins, committed by man almost from carelessness. These were what ultimately transformed loyal and holy congregations into ones far from our Torah and religion. These are what will soon totally uproot far more of Israel's great congregations, those that call themselves "moderate" or some similar name. In just a little while, another year or two, they too will be precariously perched on the brink. Then will our brothers realize that Judaism includes neither Ethical Culture,[9] nor liberalism, nor conservatism, nor three, four, five, or six other extremes. Two paths alone lie before the Jewish people: light and darkness, truth and falsehood, good and evil, life and death. Veer to one side and perish from the cold, the snow, the ice—from eternal darkness. Walk on the other side, and live a life of light, truth, morality, discipline, rest—and eternal peace.

We have two Judeo-German [Yiddish] journals in this city. Both alike are wholesome and valuable, edited by men of understanding and knowledge, men fully cognizant of the responsibilities before them. Using good, clear language, they tell us everything about Jews in all the diaspora lands. They are a beacon to both the moral and the political situation of our brethren here. They report on the good and the bad, what Jews do among themselves and what is done to them—all in complete detail.

The *Yidishe Gazeten* [Jewish Gazette] has appeared for eight years now and has proved most beneficial to Jews in this city and land. Thousands of Jews who understand no other language read it with love. Those with wisdom and understanding take it willingly as well: they most enjoy reading the articles from the pen of that skillful writer, the regular editor of this journal [Kasriel Sarasohn[10]]. He made an honorable name for himself in Hebrew style. He serves up an equally delicious fare in the vernacular. When the spirit moves him, his style flows floridly as from an inexhaustible fountain or an endless sea. His sharply eloquent words cut to the quick. Are his views always reliable and properly refined? This is not the place to probe and criticize; still, he can at least glory in that his views do not change to conform with the spirit of the day. He is not dragged along by his readers, writing for them merely what they want to hear. Instead, much to his credit, he remains faithful to the path that he set down for himself back when he first began to appear on the stands.

The *New Yorker Judische Zeitung* is only in its second year. Yet it has already succeeded in winning for itself a splendid reputation and a circulation of thousands. Its honorable editor [Dr. Morris Wechsler[11]] is not only a master of language, but also an accomplished Jewish scholar and a pious man. His goal is to stand in the breach—to chart a path to God through this vast wilderness and desert—and he fulfills this mission truthfully and faithfully. Not for a single issue has he faltered. Rather, from the day he began his work until now, he continues to fight God's battles. With fiery language, purity of faith, and wonderful piety, he time and again rouses our brethren from their slumbers. He speaks directly to their hearts, urging them to rise and unite in friendship, in order to build up from the ruins and resurrect the fallen tabernacle of our Torah. His words flow from the soul, and find their mark. Both in this city and in the state, he has performed many valuable deeds.

What displeases us about these periodicals are the many large ads that invariably cover them. Their place should be on the edges, in a corner or in some special section [see Author's Note B] as is customary in other periodicals. Instead they share prominence with excellent and important articles. The place of the richest and strongest advertisers is at the top, above some large open space. From there they spout forth, writing about what is good and bad, pleasant and unpleasant, beautiful and ugly, sacred and profane—anything about which the advertiser wishes to sound off. Most are full of exaggerations and hyperbole, unfounded statements that merely arouse mirth and loathing in all readers who follow a straightforward and honest path. We cannot understand this: Why should Jewish periodicals become centers of libertinism where every man can write just what he pleases? Why for two bits should every hypocrite and swindler be handed a forum in which to expound on delusions, frauds, and lies that wring the heart of every straightforward and honest man? We cannot say which astonishes us more: the great patience of the editor or the enormous audacity of the advertiser.

A couple of months ago we read an advertisement in one of the periodicals that was printed only in part; the rest remained in the letter file of the editor (where we were privileged to see it). Were we to judge the character and level of the ad's writer from this text, we would consider him one of the giants of the generation: a walking encyclopedia filled with worldly knowledge; a philosopher who grew up on Kant and ranks if slightly below him certainly on a level with [Moses] Mendelssohn; the world's greatest expert on languages, particularly French, Greek, English, and Italian, which he speaks like a native, and German, Hebrew, Aramaic, and Arabic, which he knows inside out. In short, a man who by virtue of his vast erudition deserves to lecture in a university hall before

24,000 students. What does such a great man want from a Jewish periodical that circulates largely in dark alleys inhabited by smallminded people of limited intelligence, whose collected wisdom is not even a drop in the bucket compared to his? Read this ad!—or better yet, ask the editor, and he'll tell you. What is this man really like? Healthy, tall, stout, and as poor in money as in mind. A great big charlatan—like so many others here in America.[12]

The publisher holds no authority over advertisements. As many readers know, the advertising department is separate, quite apart from the periodical itself. It has many fathers: the person who gathers ads from the outside, the printer who sits by his machine, the worker engaged in the "holy service" of layout, and the young typesetter. All participate; all take personal interest in their work. Many ads come to the press ready to print, complete with their lies and distortions. They are printed exactly as written; the editor may not change a word. Many ads run unaltered day after day. The editor ignores them until, at month's end, he has to pay his workers and assistants. Those who realize this will never believe or depend upon an ad, but will, rather, consider them all to be thoroughly worthless.

Many innocent readers, however, do not understand this at all. They are totally ignorant of newspaper publishing, and do not realize that it involves both editing and selling—that it is a business. They know only THE NEWSPAPER. To them it is a total universe. They believe its every word devoutly. So what can be done? Can we purposely mislead thousands of Jews? If you say that business as a whole is a mistake, a lesson in cunning, what do you say about a business that affects the soul instead of the pocketbook? Better to stop asking so as not to trouble the honorable editors about a matter that they cannot improve. They know and feel as badly about the problem as we do, but they have to hold the line at this evil: it is a disease that cannot be cured. For Jewish periodicals in America are not read by subscribers alone; indeed the readers are numerous, but the subscribers few. So most income derives from ads, particularly *kashrus* ads. Without them they would stop publishing. To tell them to stop printing ads, therefore, is to tell them to put down their pens and cease business forever.

There is one other Yiddish periodical in this city [*New Yorker Yidisher Folkstsaytung*], but we have not previously considered it out of deference to the other honorable journals mentioned. To be honest, we've never seen even a single copy of this journal; all we know about it is from hearsay, based on what some subscribers and readers have told us. Not because of its price or rarity have we avoided it; indeed, it is available in every corner newsstand in the Jewish section for what is considered to be a small sum: three cents. The reason is simply that we don't wish to see it. We often pass by the place from where its beguiling light shines forth, but our evil inclination has never tempted us to pick it up in order to examine it carefully. We've already heard enough about it. We know its methods, its purpose, its very essence, and we are disgusted even without seeing it. So we have forbidden ourselves to read it; we don't want to see it—ever.

This periodical, which we understand already has many readers and *kashrus* ads, has appeared for six months. It is written in broken Yiddish and edited by two wild kids [Moses Mintz and A. Braslavsky],[13] members of the Russian Nihilists. Their aim is to breathe fire into the hearts of Jewish workers who have heretofore shown exemplary tolerance; to arouse hatred and dissatisfaction among those laborers of our people who have always been peaceful, quiet, and satisfied; and to sow animosity and discord among the poor of the nation against the rich and well-to-do. In general they want to provoke disputes between men and their brothers. They seek to widen intellectual cleavages, incite workers to war, put an end to peace and harmony, and open Jews' eyes to nihilism—one of the few forbidden teachings that up to now has not forged inroads into the Israelite camp.

We know nothing about the actual order they propose, not even whether it conceives of a central method and purpose or is, rather, one of many nineteenth-century slogans: a word of no substance, a castle built on air. We know not whether they want to destroy the system already in our own day or only to lay the foundation for the future—after the whole world returns to a chaotic state. To us it makes no difference. Perhaps the numerous powerful enemies of this group exaggerate its sins many times over. Perhaps it is innocent of the charges we've heard. Perhaps our lips sin in calling it merely a gang of traitors and sinners—the designation employed by most people. Perhaps the group conceals some deep secret, hidden from the rest of us, particularly those of us who have no dealings with it and no expertise in its literature. And perhaps these youths have not even totally left their senses, and still have brains in their heads. This, however, we know with absolute certainty: these youths have left our sphere. They are no longer part of us, and have stopped being Jews. Were this not the case, if they felt in their breasts even one flicker of love for their people, if they felt any anxiety at all about the evil that their plans might bring down upon us, if even one drop of ancestral blood or the blood of our persecuted and crushed brethren in enemy lands flowed in their veins, then they would tremble in their boots before bringing such a terrible scourge upon Israel. Don't our enemies do well enough with the old charges and accusations? Don't they burden us with enough fictitious, undocumented claims? Need these rebellious troublemakers come and give them written cause to oppress us? Aren't the troubles we now face in this land—watching as most of our children grow distant, assimilate, and conform to foreign ways—sufficient? Will these people now come and also cut them off from the land of freedom, ensuring their destruction in two worlds at once?

The current party struggles and internal divisions consuming Israel are bad enough; shall these people now come to splinter us further, to increase our inner turmoil, to break the last of our binding ties? These good-for-nothings are not worth battling; they're not even worth talking about. We hope soon ardently to hear that this entire abortion is over and done with, dead, without leaving any trace behind. May peace reign over Israel and all mankind forever.

7 Bookstores and Religious Articles

We have five bookstores here. Two of them [Kantrowitz and Sakolski] are long-standing and have made their owners rich. Three others [Germansky, Friedman, and Drukerman[14]] are new this decade, and their owners are already filled up with work. The business is booming; it daily expands. Until a few years ago sales consisted mostly of Torah scrolls, Bibles, regular and high holiday prayerbooks, and other ritual objects. One found only a tiny number of the special books needed by those learned in Torah. But as the Jewish population increased, its need for books grew apace. Today one finds in these stores various editions of the Talmud and *poskim* [basic Jewish legal literature], as well as numbers of commentaries, responsa, novellae, legends, homilies, scholarly and literary works, and Chassidic books. This cheers us considerably, though business in these books is still insubstantial, and the number of those who seek to buy them remains small. We nevertheless see this development as a sign of change. New faces are coming here, many of them men of substance. Perhaps there is hope.

These aside, we have here many peddling book salesmen. They either work out of packs and baskets, or sell from windows and balconies in their home. They earn a meager livelihood, and that only with great difficulty.

Before the high holidays, the number of bookdealers increases; they appear in every nook and cranny of the Jewish district. Many people who peddle, beg, or work in factories the whole year round throw down their tools and engage in the sale of books needed for these days of penitence, volumes like *Sha'arei Tsiyon, Sha'arei Tefilah, Likutei Tsvi, Machzorim, Selichos, Techinos* [penitential literature, high holiday prayerbooks, penitential prayerbooks, women's prayerbooks], as well as many other similar things that our Jewish brothers and sisters need during this holy season.

This is a new phenomenon in New York, never known before. Only a few years ago it never occurred even to a poor peddler who tried his luck with twenty kinds of merchandise a week to sell books, for he knew that most New York Jews are crowded close to one another and live not far from the large book dealers, who if necessary can lower their prices at will. But one tried and succeeded, a few others followed in their footsteps, and now they number at least twenty. If competition continues to grow in like fashion, the business will soon prove unprofitable: "he who earns anything will earn it for a leaky purse" [Haggai 1:6].

In like fashion, the number of merchants selling *esrogim* [citrons for Tabernacles] and *matsos* [unleavened bread for Passover] has also increased greatly in recent years, and the competition is now exceedingly great. This has brought with it a certain amount of good. In New York any Jew can now easily observe these *mitsvos* [commandments] in the strictest possible fashion, without worrying about spending more than he can afford. Only a few years ago, a poor man in New York could not buy a *lulav* [palm branch for Tabernacles] and *esrog* of his own; even the most highly Orthodox had to observe the commandments with *esrogim* circulated around every [Tabernacles] morning [except Sabbath] by poor peddlers. Now it is hard to find any kosher traditional home without an *esrog* of its own. In many synagogues, especially the small ones, there are as many *esrogim* as worshipers.

The same is true of Passover *matsos*. Until a short while ago, most New York Jews used *matsos* made from ordinary market-quality flour, relying upon religious indulgences established for emergency conditions. Then several people arose who showed that there was no emergency whatsoever; all that was needed was some willpower. In America, after all, anything is possible. So they struggled, toiled, institutioned changes, and finally saw their work bear fruit. Soon others followed in their footsteps. Now every pious, God-fearing Jew can eat properly kosher *shmurah matsos* on Passover [*matsah* made from flour that was watched from the time it was reaped to ensure its remaining dry], and at only a slight additional cost. It is hoped that in a few years *matsos* from ordinary market-quality flour will be abandoned by Jews completely.

We know that there are many among us who complain bitterly about these "go-betweens" whose innovations permit the masses to perform religious duties. They claim, based on long acquaintance with these people, that their aims stem not from a holy desire to remove obstacles to observance, but rather from a materialistic desire to benefit themselves. Yet those who say such things are wrong. They do not realize that if American Jews had undertaken only those projects that interested the pure, God-fearing settlers without ulterior motives then we would not have here, God forbid, even a single place for communal prayer. We would also lack the few good things that Judaism in this city and land depend upon. Our view, therefore, is different: we are grateful to these people, and salute them with a "well done!"

Would that we had more *mitsvah* merchants interested in benefiting themselves. Would that new merchants would arise for the many other biblically related precepts that involve capital outlay. Just bring about urgently needed improvements; we will never ask about motivations.

The story is told of one immigrant who arrived here and barely supported himself and his wife by renting a small grocery on one of the streets. Came the month of Nisan [the Hebrew month in which Passover falls] and he did as he and all faithful Jews always did: he searched through everything that might contain *chomets* [leaven], and slowly began to remove it to the basement and attic in order to make room for the Passover goods that he had ordered a month before. On the morning before Passover, the merchandise arrived, all properly weighed and measured just as he had requested in his letter to the dealer. But to his great astonishment, no Passover certification appeared: not from the head of the *bes din*, not from some individual *dayan* [judge], not from anybody at all. He was brokenhearted—and furious. "Surely some horrible error has occurred," he cried angrily. "Doubtless some confused clerks are to blame." But what could he do? There was no time to go out to obtain new holiday merchandise, for customers had already gathered and were coming in. If sent away empty-handed, they would never return.

There remained but one solution: to race to the nearest grocers and to borrow the needed merchandise, or actually to purchase it from them at full price. This proved impossible, however. To a man, the grocers claimed that they had enough only for their own needs, and had to look out for themselves. And so, while his wife stood full of misery in the store, he ran around town like a madman. Half a day passed in turmoil and confusion. Finally they closed their doors.

Four days later, even before light had dawned on the first of the intermediate days of the holiday, he was already standing at the large supply house on S—— Street. Still enraged and furious, he fought with the supervisors and those higher up. They swore to have sent him everything he needed for Passover, but to no avail. They showed him a special place on the first floor where a sign on the wall read PASSOVER G[ROCERIES], and there was his name.

"But where is the Passover certification?"

Finally the owner of the supply house came out, brought him to his office, gave him a seat, and in a soft, earnest voice said, "I see, my friend, that you are as green as can be. You just arrived in this country, and you know nothing of its ways. Be aware of the fact that, aside from flour, there is no Passover merchandise in New York. Many Jews who would never dream of drinking c[offee] or eating s[ugar], or dried fruit on Passover, and who place in their store windows and advertisements large signs reading PASSOVER G[ROCERIES] are actually lying. The words are a deception and fraud. Since many of the storekeepers who do business with us requested it, we were forced to act as you saw. Not that it helps us any, but—as you too now understand and will know for the future—it does benefit the storekeepers in the Jewish areas."

A new year came, and he knew what lay ahead. Though snow still covered the earth, he already had a sign prepared in gold letters ready to hang in the window before the holiday. But his wife, who came from a good family in the Hungarian state, felt most distressed and argued with him daily. "How is it possible," she asked him, "to stock s[ugar] on Passover without any proper certification? Did the sages in our country dwell on this problem in vain? Did the *gaon* from Szerem waste his time troubling himself about it? And what about the dried fruits: do you know where they came from? Would the Jews back home have used them? Does America have a special Torah for itself?" Her husband listened and proceeded to burn his sign before her eyes. Now he is among those working to bring about improvements in those matters where the Torah strictly demands proper Passover supervision.[15]

We have in this city quite a number of ritual scribes. But only a few of them actually engage in holy work, for all the Torah scrolls come from Russia, Poland, and Hungary, and are sold by booksellers, while the pay for *mezuzos* and *megilos* is low. Most of them are handled by booksellers too. As for phylacteries, there isn't much business in them in America.

The only way ritual scribes can make an extra dollar is through writing
gitin [bills of divorce]—they are very common.

I see, dear reader, that you look upon me with amazement. A
question forms on your lips: Don't boys by the hundred celebrate every
year their *bnei mitsvah,* amid enormous splendor and great show? Yet you
say that there isn't much business in phylacteries, and that ritual scribes
have no work to engage in! Let me implore you, my friend, to leave me
alone. Don't press me to reveal everything to you at once. Go away! It will
be better for both of us if you don't ask! But in order that you not go away
with nothing, I'll tell you in a whisper: in many Jewish houses here the
boys reverse the usual order. They put on phylacteries before their *bar
mitsvah.* Since theirs is not a commandment performed at its usual time,
they don't go to the trouble of buying choice goods, but make do with
old ones.

I know of one important man here who on the day when his son
became *bar mitsvah,* donated a fine Torah scroll, complete with magnificent dress, to the *bes midrash.* He also held a great reception to which
he invited presidents, ex-presidents, and future presidents, as well as
many preachers, lecturers, and good friends. All delivered wisdom-filled
speeches. They thanked God who, in His abundant compassion, did
marvelous things, and left each generation with remnants—men of
extraordinary merit—who sacrificed their hearts and souls on the altar of
Torah and faith. They then proceeded to laud the *bar mitsvah* boy's
mother, teachers, and the boy himself, particularly his *maftir* [the weekly
prophetic portion] "and especially the speech which was glorious and
excellent." They praised the entire family, and held it up as an example
for all Israel. Seeing such a reception for the first time, I did not fail to
enjoy it. I left happy and in good cheer.

Next day I was called to come to the house again. I found the boy's
teacher sitting alone with the *bar mitsvah,* and trying to instruct him as
before. After reading out to him the first morning blessings, and kissing
the *tsitsis* [ritual fringes] that lay on the table, the teacher went, removed
from an old case a pair of aged phylacteries with torn, patched straps,
and asked the boy to try them on. How shocked I was to hear the little
Yankee's answer: "It is enough, the *bar mitzvah* is over already and that's
all. Let me just say the *shmoneh esreh* [eighteen benedictions]." The teacher
was in no way surprised (doubtless he was used to this), and he tried to
pacify the boy, urging him to yield for the sake of his parents. He,

however, put his own interests first, saying: "I don't care, I don't like these straps in any case."

His mother and father came into the room and, upon hearing the argument, they told the teacher to forbear: "He is a bad boy, let him go." But, though he won his battle, the lad remained bitter. After his parents left the room, he apologetically told the teacher, "My brothers, Charlie, Dave, John, Mike, and Jack all refused to put such straps on their heads and arms—why should I be called a bad boy?" And, indeed, the child was right. Just let him grow up a bit, and he will repay his parents sevenfold for their sin.

Now, gentle reader, are you still amazed that the phylacteries business in America is not very large?[16]

8 *Mohalim* and Marriage Officiators

The number of *mohalim* [ritual circumcisers] and marriage officiators [*mesadrei kidushin*] in this city are as numerous as the stars in the sky. This is not work done by communal rabbis and judges; instead, every ne'er-do-well, every bitter, unemployable man in tight straits, every lazy good-for-nothing, and everyone who in general likes to torment people becomes a marriage officiator, a job requiring neither learning nor skill, though it pays handsomely, is untaxed by the government, and is unlicensed. The gracious government intervenes neither in the affairs of the community nor in personal matters. It makes only two laws: a marriage officiator must register every marriage at a government office in writing, and must be a reverend or minister. How easy it is to secure titles in America! One of the excellent laws here holds that all who want to carry a title may come and do so.

The business of marriage officiation, which never supported anyone in the cities of our homeland, has brought many people here into a great deal of money. Many live comfortably from the work, for this is a great city, and the numbers of our Jewish brethren increase from day to day. And the person who has not yet attained wealth, who complains that this business cannot support him? His luck must have been bad, or perhaps he is the poor scion of a good family, or only a mere boy, a learned idler ignorant of the ways of the world. He hasn't discovered that this, the new world, is a world turned upside down. People walk on their heads in Columbus's land, not on their feet. All of the beautiful things that brought one fame and honor in Russia and Hungary count for nothing here. In America one must employ new and different means to

attain a good life. Here, a *mohel* or marriage officiator must be conscious
of the world around him, and the work ahead of him. He must know
how to drive a chariot properly, how to select surefooted horses, and how
to find two or three of those transient characters known as *nosei kelim*
(armor-bearers). He must understand that nothing is more valuable or
useful in America than smooth talk and vulgarity. He must realize that in
New York, unlike the rest of the world, one spends even what one does
not have. He who thoroughly understands all of this may be sure of a
place in this world: he will gather great riches and never find himself
without means of support. His lot will always be better than that of the
laborer, the peddler, and the merchant—or indeed, all of them put
together.

We ought properly to delight in the opening up of this new source
of revenue. Many valuable learned Jews in our midst earn their bread
this way. Were this field closed to them, and only opened to rabbis, as is
customary in most countries, then numerous worthy people would be
unable to support themselves, and would go around hungry and bereft
of all. Still, these people are completely ill-suited for jobs like these,
which properly require spirit and stature. This is even more true of the
average Tom, Dick, and Harry in the field, who does not lay claim to
learning, but takes on this job merely to survive, to save his family from
starvation. In our opinion it would be better for such people to find all
their paths blocked, so they would be forced to return to their homelands. Their need for support can simply not justify the horribly injurious and terribly destructive damage wrought by the anarchy that
currently reigns among the Jews in this city.

In the German magazine, A——, which is published in M——, a
certain writer agreed to publish portraits of Jewish life here. When he
came to this subject he wrote:

> The *mohalim* and marriage officiators in America's holy city
> of New York are generally unfit for their lines of work:
> they lack both the necessary expertise and the appropriate
> lifestyle. It is enough to mention that they do not consider it
> a violation for married women to go around with uncovered
> hair. Indeed, their own wives cavort like all daughters of the
> land. Many of them are not at all scrupulous about the laws
> of the Sabbath—the prohibitions on carrying, handling
> certain items, and conducting business—though these have
> always been seen as among the key aspects of the Jewish

religion. Here in our country [Germany], such creatures
would be barred from even coming close to holy work. But
there [in America] they are called "reverends," which is to
say rabbis, and they preach at every circumcision about
the holiness of the Torah and its commandments, and at
every wedding about the holiness of Jewish matrimony,
family purity, and modesty.

He concludes that such contradictions can be seen only in America—a
place where all is money and humbug. How disgraceful!

The words of this honorable writer are most dear to us. Sad to say,
he hits the nail on the head. Still, we cannot help but point out to the
honorable writer that he made three mistakes:

1. If he condemned the fools and lightweights, why could he not
say even a word about the good and honorable among them? Such an
expert in the doings of our brethren here must surely know that many
among them are men of dignity, God-fearers, and people of quality who
deserve far better positions than they have.

2. The masses in New York do not view *mohalim* and marriage
officiators as rabbis. Nor are they seen as pious, saintly men, concerned
only about *mitsvos*. Everyone knows, and they themselves admit, that they
are merchants, just like everybody else, only their merchandise is a circumcision and a marriage certificate. And if they do preach occasionally—like one unnamed reverend, a man of great mind and memory,
who has but one sermon, which he has carried around in his pocket for
ten years, never deviating from it even to the extent of changing one
word—well, what's the sin of that? Doesn't everyone preach in America?
Don't tailors and shoemakers give sermons, though everyone continues
to do as he pleases? Why should anyone be affected by what a *mohel* or
marriage officiator says? The important thing is that they don't live,
heaven forbid, off other people; they support themselves, and they even
own their own homes.

3. If he wants to castigate our brethren in New York, why did he
single out marriage officiators and *mohalim?* There are better people here,
even some with bigger certificates, who are lax about some of the things
that our author mentioned. As for covering the hair of women, only two
in a thousand observe it here. Most Jews have all but forgotten that there
are any regulations regarding this matter at all.

We ourselves shall not expand on these themes now. The proper
time has still to come. But how sweet were the sounds of the writer's last

words: "Such contradictions can only be seen in America . . . " How true, dear writer, how very true![17]

Far be it from us to judge the actions of New York's *mohalim* and marriage officiators in the manner employed recently by one of the best writers here. He fell upon them in undisguised fury, robbed them of all honor, and did not hesitate to call many prominent *mohalim,* whom he mentioned by name, "troublemakers in Israel," and many New York marriage officiators "harder on Israel than the generation of the flood."

Heaven preserve us from slandering a large congregation in Israel! We know that they do not fail on purpose. All the difficulties named by the author mentioned above stem not from malice, recklessness, or lack of faith, heaven forbid. We are certain that they acted unintentionally, and did not know in advance all the things that were revealed to them later on. If, for example, John Doe the *mohel* had known when he circumcised the "great Gentile" and brought him into the covenant of Abraham that he did not truly accept the burdens of Torah and faith, and that his sole intention was to bring under his wing a virgin daughter of Israel and her three hundred in cash, then he surely would have forgone the honor, forgone the $25, forgone officiating at the nuptial arrangements, and forgone the marriage itself. Indeed, he would have had no dealings with the man whatsoever.

If only a certain *mohel* had known when he circumcised without properly uncovering the membrane of the corona or without sucking the wound three times that his friends would reprove him and force him to perform the circumcision again. If only he had known that they, being God-fearing men of truth, aimed not to provoke him or to give him a bad name or to hurt his business, but only to have things done properly as set forth in the Torah. Surely he would not have then tried to hush things up but would, rather, have joined in the effort to make amends, for he would not have wanted to assume the responsibility of having caused uncircumcised Jews to grow up in Israel.

If only a certain *mohel* had known that when he received payments (which his hands didn't manage to remove from his pocket) on the Sabbath at a postcircumcision reception held at one poor man's house, or when he was forced to accept his payment from guests who pay only on the day [of the reception, the Sabbath notwithstanding], that this would lead to gossip, and that his actions would be revealed in the press leading to a desecration of God's name. Surely he would then have passed up the $5 he collected, and would not have performed this abomination, which transformed his blessing into a curse and practically robbed him of his means of support. Had he but caught on, as all must who have eyes in their heads, to how life is in America!

If only a certain marriage officiator who read loudly from the *kesubah* [marriage certificate], "Menasheh son of Joseph, the groom said to this virgin" and then performed the marriage according to the rites of Judaism, really knew that the groom was from birth a complete non-Jew: born naturally circumcised, neither converted nor immersed in a ritual bath, never having appeared before a Jewish court.

If only a certain reverend who waxed enthusiastic under a wedding canopy in praise of the bride and her sterling qualities really knew that this beauty already had a husband in London, and that this groom was actually her "second mate."

If only a certain marriage officiator, truly an important God-fearing man, really knew when he opened the reading of the *kesubah* with customary joy and merriment, that he was standing "between the straits," just a few days before the fast of the Ninth of Av, when all Israel properly sits in mourning, and marriage is forbidden.

If only all those reverends here who have fallen into performing improper marriages really knew that they had been deceived and caught in a trap. If only some person came along, even a non-Jew or a minor, and whispered this to them quietly, even as late as the marriage or the payment, we don't hesitate to say that the effect would be that of a thunderclap close at hand. Gripped by fear, they would escape as if from an avalanche, and run in fright to hide out for three days, leaving behind the wedding canopy, the fee, the bride, the groom, the in-laws, the bridal party, and all the guests. For they are truly good, upright Jews. But man, when endangered, worries about his income, and nobody's income in New York is more insecure than that of a marriage officiator. Twenty, even 120, jump for every job. If one marriage officiator delays, pending investigations and inquiries, a second no less important a man will run to snatch the role out of his hands. And if he too deliberates overly long, a third person will instantly come and pull gold from their ruins. In the end, somehow or other, the abominable deed will be done.

Assuming that what we say is correct, and that those who err don't do so intentionally, how does this help us? Won't the same good intentions lead them astray in the future? Will the competition for jobs cease? Will it not cause the same errors to recur again and again? So what will become of the Torah, family purity, and modesty? Do we really have here a world of lawlessness? Will all suggestions and tactics for changing the face of things come to naught? How very much have we fallen! How horrible our condition! Terrible! Frightful!

9 Beggars and Charity

In this industrious city we have hundreds of *batlanim* [idlers], people who eat but do not work. These are not *batlanim* of the sort praised by our rabbis when they required every city in Israel to have at least ten of them [for purposes of worship and study]. These are true *batlanim;* lazy people who revel in idleness and relish the unearned bread of charity. Their entire work and livelihood comes from visiting and begging; they throw themselves at the mercy of the community, and hate with a passion any form of labor or industry.

Until four or five years ago, New York beggars met with great success in their work and made good money. A few even became merchants or returned to their homelands. All found enough to feed their families. We know many whom God had blessed with lots of sons and daughters, all healthy and hardworking, some of whom gave up half of all their salaries so that [their fathers], the old *batlanim,* would not be in need of anything and might even have a dollar left over to put away and save. But knowing that they were in America, a country where one must not sit idle, they decided that they too might set their hands to work.

In those days in New York, begging was the best work there was. On its account tailors gave up their needles, and peddlers their packs. Those accustomed to begging from their youth, who were so to speak pedigreed for exceptional "house-guesting" abilities, never ceased to complain about their early travails. They wondered at their own foolish stupidity in having spent the best and healthiest days of their youth wandering from village to village and town to town in poor countries where men sat in the dark. The bright idea never occurred to them to

travel to America where begging was a nice, pleasant, and most wonderful experience—especially in the blessed city of New York where
more Jews live in a single block than in an entire large city in Poland, and
more in one house than in ten whole villages in Lithuania and Hungary.
A beggar in New York could carry on his business in a simple and
honorable manner, without expending a great deal of effort. He could go
out in the morning and return home in the afternoon having accomplished more in four hours than he did in three full days and a journey of
nearly forty miles in his homeland. He could be a big shot, a respectable
person in the community. Most important of all, he could make money
and become a *parnas*.

But the early beggars were fools. They couldn't keep their mouths
shut, and soon revealed the secret to others. They drew after them all the
beggars from G[ermany] and from other countries where this kind of
business flourished. For three years they continued to arrive in waves:
schooled beggars all, confirmed houseguests, full of experience. Now-
adays, just as is true in other professions, so too in begging the competition has grown and business has fallen—dramatically. Although our
Jewish brethren remain fully as merciful as always they were, and have
never forgotten the law requiring them to assist all who stretch out their
hands in need, still the number of visitors and door-to-door beggars has
exceeded the limit. In spite of every good intention and charitable spirit,
they cannot do justice to them all. Any beggar who doesn't understand
the minute details of his work, who doesn't know to change his plea
constantly, to disguise himself, to be always somebody else—once
dumb, once suffering, once blind, once lame; who doesn't realize that
merely to lower eyes and stretch out hands no longer suffices to collect
money enough to live on, but that one must rather follow many others
and begin to shout and wail—he had better stay put in his own country
and never come to America at all.

We won't shed a tear about this. Would that all idlers came to
realize that begging in America is a worthless enterprise. Would that they
all returned home en masse in a boat, leaving just the truly impoverished
and unfortunate, who really cannot work. Then Jewish money would no
longer flow to those who, by taking money, deprive the truly poor, those
who previously—until these men came and snatched the bread out of
their mouths—had always been supported.

This charity work—to give aid to every wayfarer and all who stretch
out their hands—provides little benefit, and serves no laudable end of
the sort that all Israel might exalt in (see Author's Note C). It rather

causes cheaters and idlers to multiply. Ultimately the burden falls only on the truly poor, who are far more needy.

Our rich brethren generally live hidden away behind impregnable mansions where one cannot reach them, much less speak to them, without first ringing "Their Highness' bell" and announcing oneself to the servants. Needy visitors recognize at once that the servants and bell are not made to honor them. Their stomping grounds are generally confined to dark alleys, Jewish quarters, and poorer sections with large tenements and dreary open courtyards. There unfortunate peddlers and workers live. Every penny they earn comes at the expense of their own sweat and blood.

The subject is of itself very ugly. Is it not a horrible disgrace that in a labor-filled city like this, where all the inhabitants young and old alike work so hard and even little children toil strenuously in order to feed themselves; in a city where the old, the weak, the students, the wise men, and the writers cannot depend on others but must support themselves— that in such a city hundreds of people wander through the courtyards and marketplaces without anybody noticing? That in this city beggary has found a home and grows ever stronger in horrible fashion? Yes, it is a disgrace, a disgrace to all Israel. The subject has received sufficient attention in the periodicals. Many have blamed our philanthropic brethren for the evil's spread. For had they not been so openhearted but instead been more careful of believing every vain and light fellow who aroused their mercy—following the example of our brethren in Germany and many Russian and Polish cities—then begging would already have stopped in New York and would by now be only a memory.

All of these things are true. We cannot blame writers for their bitter words when they report facts. Still, these acts of charity remain dear and honorable to us, in spite of all the deficiencies connected with them. We cannot follow the counsel of those who want to cut off the benevolent hand at its source. With all due respect to our dear writers, theirs are incautious words motivated by anger. They seek to throw the baby out with the bathwater.

[Dear writers] we know about all the faults you mention in the current charity system, as well as you do. What we have already written should suffice to show that we know as well as you do that many of the poor deserve no sympathy and that to aid them is really a crime. But we also know that there are many who are truly poor and destitute; every penny given them is an act of eternal righteousness. We know that many of the poor retain their pride and find begging at the door of philanthropists to be mortally bitter. To have poverty in one's household is awful, worse than all the plagues and torture in the world, worse even than death. In the end who will assume the responsibility to decide between truth and falsehood? Who has the power to sift out the cheaters? Will we probe and investigate every visiting beggar, clutching our penny to our breast until we are sure of his entire life's story? Will we, as you suggest, abandon everything and give nothing to anyone? That would be folly and mean-spirited: How can you destroy an old system if you have nothing with which to replace it? We form but a small part of the world; dare you threaten even that?

The fact that many European Jewish communities did as you suggested in your article and abandoned the system of charity proves nothing. Before replacing the destructive system of community-wide begging which so disgraces and humiliates us in the eyes of our Gentile neighbors, they took proper preventive measures. They prepared a better system centered around soup kitchens, general charity funds, benevolent, free-loan and clothing societies, hospitals, orphanages, bridal and circumcision funds, and similar precious things that bring Jews praise from all over the world. But sadly for all those who love their religion and people, the Orthodox Jews here in our midst have not created a single one of these. Except for the *landsmanschaften,* synagogues, *chazanim,* and the benevolent, insurance and benefit societies, we have nothing, nothing at all.

There are, to be sure, those charity societies that we mentioned in chapter I and promised to talk about, with God's help, in a separate essay. We termed them charity and benevolent societies because of their great value to so many poor people. But they have no connection at all with the societies that we have just mentioned. For with them charity is only paid out at the end, essentially as repayment of a loan. Those who contributed nothing to the fund receive nothing. As you will see, dear reader, in the pamphlet that, with God's help, I shall publish when this pamphlet is done, even a contributor has great difficulty if, heaven forbid, he needs a bit of charity during his lifetime. If his fortune changes and he needs a small part of his principal—except if he happens to have served as chairman or as a member of the ruling board—and if he doesn't know the rules of reciprocal favors, then he will receive a lesson in true American brotherhood. Any complaint will be answered with the cry of "Silence—friends and neighbors are badly off too, and if each will demand a small part of his principal. . . . "

But hark! The treasurer has his book open: "For two quarters you have made no additional payment to your account." So instead of receiving his principal back, the erstwhile contributor is dismissed that very night from the society. Membership, fellowship, and fraternal love all cease instantly. The bonds of friendship dissolve forever.

Recently, I attended a private meeting of the board of one of these societies, and I had the good fortune to come early—something which I haven't done in a long time, since business keeps me too busy to come and go as I please. The meeting opened as usual with the sweet homily that is printed on page one of the larger organization's book of common rituals. The president, an enlightened tailor, appended to this another string of pearls: a reading of many biblical and rabbinic passages, which originated, according to his own admission, in the German translation of the *Menoras Hame'or* ["Candlestick of Light" (1514), by Isaac Aboab]. From the same valuable source he borrowed his closing thought, dealing with the relationship between *tsedakah* [charity] and *chesed* [goodness]. He pointed out that the word *tsedakah* comes from the word *tsedek* [justice], which is the equivalent of *yosher* [equity]. Equity means giving to all according to what they deserve. Thus when a person gives from his own money to the poor soul who is hard up because of his particular means of livelihood, that is called *tsedakah:* the man gets only what is due him. But when a man gives more, and gives even to those who are less poor but still unable completely to support themselves, or gives physical support to a friend, even a rich one, who happens to be sick or dying, or something else of this sort, that is called *chesed*, as it is written [Hosea 10:12], "Sow *tsedakah* for yourselves; reap the fruits of *chesed.*"

The assembled beloved brethren lapped these delightful words up. At the conclusion they applauded and cheered; indeed they would still be cheering today had not the president forgone the honor due him and rapped loudly for silence. Then they began their agenda for the day and eventually reached the all-too-familiar item: the secretary placed on the table a letter of request from one of the brethren, as follows:

> I, John Doe, the undersigned, have been a member of this organization for five years, and have always paid my bills on time. Thank God, I have only requested aid once last year when I received $5, and at the beginning of this year when the lodge extended $10 to me. I regret having to burden you again, but God has made my lot a bitter one and I am down to my last loaf of bread. I have nobody to whom to turn except you, my dearly beloved righteous and charitable brethren, and I hope that you will not hesitate to help me, for I have given everything I have in pledge. If, heaven forbid, you close your hands to me, I shall be reduced— heaven preserve me—to knocking on doors.

Even before the president had finished reading the letter of this unfortunate man, the members had begun to quarrel, their voices growing louder and louder until they reach a fever pitch. "Give at once," a few shouted, while others demanded that the matter be brought to judgment, and that a committee of five be dispatched. Still a third group screamed that this man was nothing but a "sucker," who had already stolen $15 from the lodge and deserved not a penny more. The quarreling and fighting lasted two whole hours and almost led to fisticuffs and rioting. Finally a vote was taken and those in favor led those opposed.

The assistant treasurer was just about to extend $8.50 in credit when suddenly a new problem arose. Up got one of the members who had just walked in, a former president, and he poured fire and brimstone on the chairman's head, asking arrogantly, "Is this the law? Why didn't the president ask the secretary, even before the deliberations began, to examine the debt register to see if this man deserves any help? Perhaps he is a second-class ["rear"] member and has no right to ask for assistance? Perhaps he is overdue and it's time for the society to expel him altogether?" The president admitted his mistake and asked the secretary to search the records. All were aghast to learn that "this very day marks the 185th day since his payments into the treasury ceased." That put an end to all arguments. The assistant treasurer put the $8.50 back into his wallet. Those favoring the petitioner buried their heads in sand. The secretary read out the offense, and punishment was meted out: the man was no longer to be a member of the organization, his name was erased from its books, and henceforward all connections with him were severed.

Greatly disappointed, the man left, never to return again. When I saw the president's joy at having been saved from committing "a sin," and the former president's joy at his personal victory, I remembered the opening homily and remarks, which I had enjoyed but a few hours earlier. Then I called to mind the case [see Shabat 55a] of the woman who cried out before [the talmudic sage] Samuel [but was ignored]. I said to myself [as Samuel said], "Your superior will be punished with cold water [remaining unscathed], but your superior's superior will be punished with hot" [for his is the higher court, which should take the matter up].

After several days I told this story to a countryman. He told me with surprise that on the very same night, just the same thing had happened in his society to a poor, honorable man who was a founding and loyal member for over eight years. Tragically his distinguished wife subsequently died, and he couldn't find people to care for her remains and bury her. So she lay for three days until people from the Eighth Street [United Hebrew Charities] took pity on her, and performed for her this last act of righteousness.

He went on to describe to me many similar stories: in his view they are everyday occurrences here. When he was done, he recited over these unfortunates a verse [from Isaiah 28:18]: "Your covenant with Death shall be annulled, you pact with sheol shall not endure." And I, the memory of that enlightened tailor's sermon fresh in my mind, completed the verse: "When the sweeping flood passes through, you shall be its victims . . . and it shall be sheer horror to grasp the message."[18]

If we destroy those charities that we have, we shall cut hundreds of people off from their last hope. Dear, honorable writers are therefore wrong [even in suggesting this]. As long as things continue to stand as they are, we have no right to tamper with our charity system for it keeps many people alive. As our truly righteous rabbis of blessed memory said [Ketubot 68a], "Come let us be grateful to rogues, for were it not for them we [who do not always give charity as we should] would have been sinning every day." The great rabbi Isaac Aboab of blessed memory adds that despite the rogues, man should not refuse charity to anyone who asks, for better it is to grant alms to one not in need than to risk denying them to one who is. Glory to those privileged to distribute what they have to the deserving poor!

Those of us downtown may be lax in charity; our philanthropic brethren uptown, however, are remarkable. Bitter as it is for us to see the breaches they have made in the great wall of religion—how, among many of them, respect for our holy Torah has fallen to a low ebb; how they view it as a glob of clay to be molded in any way they see fit; how little they have left unreformed; and how, sad to say, they have destroyed and polluted the vineyard of Israel down to its very roots—still, when it comes to charity, righteousness, and good deeds, we cannot deny them their due. We may not hide the truth: in this respect they are better than we are—ten times better. Where among us the need is great and charity disorganized, everything related to their charity is highly progressive and in wonderfully good order. Where our hands are open to all passersby and we spread our charity aimlessly with little benefit, our [uptown] brethren have strong, reliable, and beautifully built institutions. They enjoy their work and accomplishments. The fruits of their righteous labors are visible all over: charity houses for the poor, orphanages for those without parents, refuges for the elderly, infirmaries for the sick, and large impressive societies to serve every other useful and important human need. Thousands of unfortunates have had their lives saved because of them.

We copy here for the reader a list of some of the most important and best-known of these institutions:

1. Hebrew Orphan Asylum
2. Ladies' Lying-in Relief Society
3. Hebrew Benevolent Fuel Society
4. Hebrew Relief Society
5. Montefiore Home
6. Home for Aged Hebrews
7. Home for Aged Bne-Brith [B'nai B'rith]
8. Deborah Nursery
9. Bikur Cholim Society
10. Gates of Hope Ladies Benevolent Association
11. Hebrew Sheltering Guardian Society
12. Hebrew Technical Institute
13. Passover Relief Association
14. Mount Sinai Hospital

This last-mentioned hospital[19] is unique; I doubt that anything similar to it could be found in any other Jewish city. With the exception of the great institution that we shall discuss at length in the text [United Hebrew Charities], its good deeds exceed those of every other benevolent institution here. It was first established [i.e., the cornerstone was laid] in 1853, on 28th Street, by several public-spirited philanthropists. Though all now are deceased, their good names and the memory of their righteousness live on forever. As the years passed by, their charitable work was joined by many other friends, among them some of our richest brethren. Finally, in 1872, they succeeded in collecting together enough in the way of contributions to relocate. In place of a small house that was far too narrow to hold all the sick among us who required help and medical attention, they built a magnificent edifice on Lexington Avenue, which cost close to $400,000. On that spot the house still stands, majestic in its splendor, a monument to the wisdom and glory of Israel in this city and land.[20]

The most important and praiseworthy of all the organizations engaged in the glorious work of charity is the famous large philanthropy known as the United Hebrew Charities.[21] Like a mother bird, it spreads a protective wing over the poor of our nation. Who knows how many thousands of souls would have died from starvation or committed suicide when they fell on hard times had not this dear charity considered their plight, worried about their spirit, and rescued them? Many writers have already described this institution in books and articles. Every city in the Jewish diaspora looks upon it with respectful awe.

The United Hebrew Charities distributes annually to the poor of this city 900 to 1,000 *kar* [tons(?)] of coal, and 6,000 clothes of various kinds. It watches over many hundreds of pathetically poor pregnant women, filling all their needs. It maintains some twenty doctors and stocks necessary medicines to facilitate visits to those poor and sickly who cannot afford the care and attention that they need. It supports two large technical schools for teaching Jewish children trades. It finds employment for thousands of discouraged workers. It funds boat tickets for hundreds of people who are unhappy here and want, for whatever reason, to return to their homelands. It provides railway tickets to many poor people who want to move on and settle in other cities around this country. It distributes lodging and meal tickets to thousands of youths and distitute wanderers who trudge gloomily through the streets without work or sustenance. It assumes responsibility for burying "deserted corpses," which nobody else will bury—here that means anyone thrown out of his society, and even people who are listed on a society's "rear list" but lost their rights for not paying their bills on time. These unfortunates, if, heaven forbid, a disaster comes upon them, learn to appreciate how great this particular act of righteousness is. Most of all, it spreads the canopy of its benevolence over hundreds of needy families, which it supports. Some receive monthly stipends and are listed in the books as regulars. Others, aided only occasionally when they have a particular need, are also listed for memory's sake in the society's books. Many, many, however, are unlisted: they rove hither and yon as wandering, uninvited guests—anonymous immigrants about whom nothing is known. True, they get only little, and then only once or twice. But the number of those requesting handouts is very great.

We would sing the praises of this dear society even longer, but we see that we have much work to do in other subjects. What we have already written should in any case serve to demonstrate the greatness of its charitable and benevolent activities. Would that these philanthropists showed equal devotion to God, Torah, and religion, that their good deeds be not offset by bad ones. Then the work of *tsedakah* would be complete. The poor would have increasing joy through the Lord, and the neediest of men would exult in the Holy One of Israel [see Isaiah 29:19].

We observe with very great regret that most of our brethren here pay no attention to the great work of this society except when they seek compassion during times of trouble. Then the first name that pops into every distressed person's head is "Hebrew Charities," or "Eighth Street." But when fortune smiles upon them, they forget its existence entirely. It would never occur to them to give "The Charities" $10; they'd much prefer to join four or five different societies, though their annual cost comes to much more. How disgraceful, how shamefully embarrassing to us and all Israel that the names of our brethren from this area comprise fewer than 2 percent of the names found on the charity board's annually published list of donors, though they are the charity's primary beneficiaries; most of those who seek and receive aid come from their midst. Worse still, only four or five synagogues—out of a total, including societies, of several hundred—have seen fit to contribute. This is the reason behind the beloved society's recent attempt to have the government halt the immigration of paupers from Europe.[22] It knows that the burden of caring for such people falls entirely on its own head. Where will it find money to feed and seek jobs for these people, or send them back? Should it devote all its funds and resources to them alone, especially if it receives no support from the masses of our people, including thousands who could afford to help but stand aloof?

But enough. The time has come, dear brethren, for us to rouse ourselves, act, and accomplish something for our nation's poor—something concrete and long-lasting. It is time we took pity on the thousands of families in misfortune, time we tried to ease their plight. If we cannot yet succeed in gathering together the forces needed to build towering philanthropic institutions of our own, is it not best to help existing charities to expand the scope of their good work? Deduct $25 from the annual salary of your *chazan*. Set aside some of the money you spend on gifts for retiring *parnasim*. Set aside just one-tenth of the sum willingly pledged to people who cannot possibly benefit Israel or the world at large—*chazanim,* wedding jesters, and the like—people whom we have mentioned above and those whom we do not wish to deal with at all. Set aside just one-hundredth of what is spent on momentary entertainment—theaters, balls, and picnics. If everyone did this, and brought this great sum of money—doubtless many tens of thousands of dollars—straight to the United Hebrew Charities, to the Mount Sinai Hospital, and to the Hebrew Orphan Asylum, then what a heartwarming sight it would be. You would see how your own efforts helped your poor brethren and gladdened the hearts of many widows, orphans, sick, wretched, and depressed people who now cower before their own poverty and hardship.

My dear modest, merciful, and charitable brethren, you would see a great and most delightful change take place in many Jewish homes. Laurel would replace ashes, festivity replace mourning, and life, hope, and comfort replace brokenheartedness, despair, and gloom. Your good deeds would become known by the Gentiles, all would hear of your righteousness, and you would be called terebinths of victory, planted by the Lord for his glory [see Isaiah 61:3].

If large numbers of our pious brethren participated and donated as much as they could to these benevolent institutions, then their honorable governors would unhesitatingly agree to changes of policy that would in every way accommodate pious, Torah-observing Jews. Hundreds who at present would never even ask to be admitted would be able to find refuge there. Now some sick and dying refrain from requesting cures for their bodies, fearing for their souls. Many, irreproachably loyal Jews who have always been careful not to contaminate themselves with [nonkosher] food or alter their holy ways and customs, especially at a time when they should be particularly careful to mind themselves and their actions, find to their sorrow that these benevolent institutions are not strict about matters of faith and Torah. If not for their names, it would, based on their policies and regulations, be almost impossible to recognize that they even were Jewish. Of course, no one can blame those unfortunates who do seek aid; there is, after all, nowhere else for them to turn.

Once I was walking on Ludlow Street, the street famous for its vast commerce in stinking fish, moldy fruit, old clothes, and similar good things that spread delicious odors to the noses of those who walk there in large numbers. As I passed in front of one of those large buildings surrounded on all sides by stores and businesses dealing in the sort of merchandise that I have described, a man selling vegetables and broken utensils approached me and asked me by name whether I knew old Mr. B.——, the *magid*. "Yes," I replied, "I know this scholarly rabbi. Do you have any news of him?"

"Bad news," he replied; "the *magid* lives here in my house, in a small attic room there on the fourth floor. He is sick and has been lying in bed for three weeks. I have already spread the word to many of the *bate midrash* [studies] where he used to preach, but nobody comes to seek him out except Mr. S.——, who runs the large business on D.—— Street. He comes to visit him occasionally, and always leaves him a good contribution. The wise Dr. P.—— is also kind enough to visit him, and he brings him medicine for free. Otherwise, not a single one of his acquaintances has come by."

This bad news was like a sharp blow to my heart. I dearly loved this honorable old man, enjoyed his company for years, and had always derived pleasure from his beautiful sermons and clever articles. It was only due to extenuating circumstances that for a long time I had not seen him. I therefore abandoned for another day what I was doing—though I was going about on business and had some pressing matters to attend—and I went to visit him. What can I tell you, dear readers? You should never have to witness the horrible scene that I witnessed in the preacher's house. I still feel shaky and faint whenever I think about the terrible sight that appeared before my eyes. The unfortunate patient tried to gather his strength, to appear peaceful, and to hide his pain. He overcame enough of his suffering to smile at me and to talk about a variety of subjects as if he lacked nothing. But I saw what was before me; I saw his squalid condition. And I became furious, like a man possessed.

As I turned to leave, I asked if he wanted me to try to find him a place in M[ount Sinai] Hospital. He shook his beard as a sign that he thought my words improper, and broke into a tearful laugh that penetrated deep into my heart, breaking it into little pieces. I asked again, "Why don't you take pity on yourself? I, a healthy man, haven't the strength to stay in this room; how can you, sir, expect to get well here?" I saw that he preferred to evade the question rather than having to explain things clearly to me, so I begged him to tell me the basis of his resolve. He answered me with difficulty and in a feeble voice: "You have done well, my friend, to see what I need. I do indeed need a clean room, fresh air, and a quiet atmosphere more than medicine. But no, this I cannot do! I know the extent of my illness; I know that the specter of death hovers over me. Every minute I think that the oppressive air will choke my soul. But I am getting old. What else can I do? The overseers there [in the hospital] are indeed goodhearted, merciful men who perform countless acts of righteousness on behalf of the wretchedly ill. But I am a Jew: a rabbi and preacher in Israel! Will I now, at the end of my life, defile myself with [nonkosher food]? How will I pray, study, and fulfill my other Jewish needs which, thank God, not even my illness has stopped me from performing? No, I cannot do it! Don't press me, my friend: don't start finding me *heterim* [permissive solutions]. I won't move from here no matter what."

Here the unfortunate man became weak and had no more strength to talk. But seeing my great sorrow, the tears rolling down my cheeks, he marshaled the last of his strength and said, "My friend, don't pity me or shed tears over my plight. I am old, wise, and used to troubles. What is the story of my life in this country if not one of frequent troubles? The Lord who has for ten years given me the strength to bear my suffering will preserve and keep me now as well. I will endure until He cures me. Then I shall be satisfied to wander as before. I swear that more than worrying and feeling sorry for myself and my own bitter plight, I worry and feel sorry about the fate of my friends—rabbis, preachers, learned men, students of Torah—who now come in droves from the cities of our homelands. What will finally become of these dear souls here? If only they had the sense now, when they've just come and still possess their strength, to throw off their rabbinic mantles and become laborers or businessmen. Let the work be what it will—transporting stones, cleaning courtyards and pathways, hawking cards, scarves, and matches, whatever—just so long as it is some kind of manual labor or trade. Would that I had thought to do this when I arrived. Had I been a peddler or tailor, instead of a preacher, lecturer, and author, I might not be lying full of pain in this room right now. It would have occurred to people to visit me and care for me. I would not have to fall as a burden on the shoulders of the poor greengrocer who is more in need of mercy than I am, though I ask him for favors. I might now be . . . "

The words vanished from his lips as his ailment took a sudden turn for the worse and he could no longer speak. I remained confused and frightened, rooted to my place. I did not know where to turn for advice. At that moment the door opened and Dr. P.—— entered the room. He took one look into the face of his patient, who lay unconscious, and turning to me, he commanded that I go at once to Mr. S.——to tell him in his name that peril was close, very close, unless he moved quickly to transport the patient out of his dank, narrow room. "If you want to see the old man alive, hurry up," he said with emphasis.

In the end the unfortunate old man was brought to a hospital—not to Lexington Avenue [Mount Sinai], but to Gouverneur Street [Hospital]. That was what the doctor ordered. It was also what his righteous benefactor wanted so that he might be able to visit him and inquire after his health. He lay there in pain, amidst the sick and wretched of various nations, for about a month, while excruciatingly bitter tortures wracked his body and soul. Now, finally, he has recovered—if not to complete health, at least to his original condition. Again he can go around from society to society, from group to group, and from *parnas* to *parnas* in search of sermon opportunities. His prophecy has come to pass: his illness is cured and he is now wearily wandering once again.

I submit this brief tale, true in its every word, to *parnasim* and all who engage in communal activities, that they might read it whenever they gather to discuss employment of a *chazan,* broadening of the seats, or decoration of the synagogue walls. Whosoever reads this tale slowly, carefully, and with feeling, will find in it a wonderful treasure.[23]

10 *Chazanim*[24]

We gave this chapter a name due to the enormous value and importance of the subject it discusses. We have frequently hinted at this subject in earlier chapters without finding the time right to expand upon it. Now our readers will be good enough to forgive us if we discuss it at length. Before us stands a matter of the greatest significance: a subject that sits at the summit of the American Jewish world. Since our brothers began to deal diligently with this—thanks to our good *parnasim*, the guardians of the city—American Jewish life has undergone a remarkable change.

We do not exactly know the number of *chazanim* to be found in this city. But one thing is absolutely certain: there are twice as many of them as there are synagogues and societies—and this does not include the innumerable small-time *chazanim* and readers who are out of touch with the spirit of the times. How all are supported by their work is a wonder. Many rent themselves out exceedingly cheaply, and the vast majority do not work steadily for any one congregation, yet even the lowliest *chazan* rarely complains that business is bad.

A steady position here serves largely as a face-saving device. One's major source of income comes through the free market. And how vast that market is here in New York! For *chazanim* and similar types it is a rich treasure-trove, an inexhaustible fountain. All can uncover its mysteries and probe its hidden secrets, provided they see what sits in front of their eyes and follow expertly all those rules and regulations that we have already mentioned in an earlier chapter.

The generosity of New Yorkers is boundlessly unlimited. Yet from among the vast multitude here, including singers and musicians of all types, many congregations last year could still not find for themselves a sweet-singing *chazan* of their liking. They had paraded before themselves almost every *chazan* in the city, one after another, like a flock of sheep. They spared no exertion, setting aside all their business and private affairs. They sat morning till night in committees, weighing the merits of the various performances and testing each candidate in various and sundry ways. But in the end, despite all their labor and effort, they did not succeed in finding among the lot even a single *chazan* who sang well enough to satisfy them. So leaders gathered in the various congregations and decided, after much debate, to introduce something new into the country. They added an additional tax on members, sought increases in pledges and gifts, ran up their budgets, and began forthwith to search for true *chazanim*—right from the source where they were raised. They sought world-famous, universally acclaimed *chazanim*—ones who would add to their luster and generally increase the glory of Israel in this land.

In the spring of 1886, when *chazanim* still had six full months to go on their contracts, and after congregations had already placed their [job] announcements in the Hebrew press, a series of advertisements, letters, and telegrams flew from place to place across the Jewish world, creating a sensation among *chazanim* everywhere. The enormous sums bandied about—$1,500, $2,000, $3,000—aroused excitement in every corner, and reached many receptive ears. The finest, most wonderful *chazanim* came over in large numbers, followed hard on their heels by a flood of unknown fledglings lured by delightful fantasies of stars falling by the wayside. They mistakenly assumed that in music, as in so many things, America would prove an upside-down world: the best would sink, the lowliest rise to the top. They shortly discovered their error. When it came to music, they found America to be a straightforward world where even Russians, Lithuanians, and Hungarians showed great powers of musical appreciation. They watched with amazement as the greatest, most illustrious *chazanim* [Israel Michalovsky and Israel Cooper]—who had served in the capital of P[aris] and in the great Jewish city of V[ilna] and were known there for decades—even these two eminents, beloved, unequaled, internationally famous as they were, still had to stand up and be tested. So did those who can properly be called musical masters, acclaimed by crowds, never forced to submit to a test in their lives—they too, with bowed heads and humbled pride, had to pass muster before wise Americans. The battles were long and arduous, but finally a compromise was reached and selections made. Undoubtedly, in another year or two, those chosen will decline in favor, and congregations will create another worldwide sensation when they seek to replace them. And so it will be, alas, year after year, back and forth, until finally a new immigration pattern becomes established: young, wandering lambs will be sought from the lands of their dispersion; old, used-up *chazanim* will be returned from whence they came fifty years earlier.

Let me faithfully describe for you, dear reader, the enormous commotion surrounding the *chazan* question during these past two years. It has brought tumult to every Jewish home, turned sons against fathers, brides against grooms, men against brothers. There is fighting over the *chazan* question all day long.

Those engaged in communal activities spend a good deal of their time—be it in synagogue, in the community house, or among street gatherings—quieting down grumblers and angrily scolding mockers who brazenly suggest that the great *chazanim* finally chosen after long and ugly battling are in fact no better than the old *chazanim* whom they replaced. The old ones were satisfied with $500—exactly a fourth the salary that the new, more famous *chazanim* command.

Parnasim, leaders of the community, treasurers, officials, and assistants must all go to a great deal of trouble every Sabbath and holiday simply to keep God's people orderly. They must police the thousands who gather from all manner of societies and organizations, pushing and shoving one against the other. They must pay careful attention to ensure that everyone sits in his appropriate seat: some to the right or left of the *parnas,* some against the eastern wall, some in the middle, and some permitted only to lean against the door. Most important of all, they must work assiduously in the hall and the courtyard. Guards and policemen must themselves be overseen, least they abuse their positions. Watchmen watch watchmen, guards and policemen oversee other guards and policemen, and everyone is shifted between the three major parts of the service, this all just to make doubly sure that nobody—neither people with means who want free entertainment at the expense of others, nor people completely without means who don't have the money to purchase entry—should, heaven forbid, be able to steal their way in [to hear the *chazan*] without a proper ticket.

Batlanim and loafers are joyful. Idleness had of late brought them to the point of boredom. Now they have ample opportunity to stretch out full length [and be entertained for hours].

The story is told of one poor peddler who had not been able to listen to any of the new, famous *chazanim* even once since he arrived in the country six months before. Finally, one Sabbath eve, desire overcame him. He took his entire fortune, all fifty of the cents that he had managed to scrape together, and purchased a standing-room place in the large M.—— Synagogue, the home of that incomparable *chazan*, Mr. Y.——.

That evening, after *Kabalas Shabas* prayers [welcoming the Sabbath] had been sung, and his soul was filled with joy, he recalled the ticket that was in his pouch. Much as it pained him to carry it outside, a violation of the Sabbath that he had never before committed, he nevertheless brought it to the synagogue *shamash* [sexton] and asked him if he would be willing to hold the ticket for him in one of the stands until the morrow. The old *shamash* laughed inwardly and readily agreed. The next morning at 8 A.M., when the man came seeking entry, he found to his utter mortification that the *shamash* to whom he had given the ticket was nowhere to be found. Naturally the doorman angrily told him to go away, but he paid no attention. Spurred by the righteousness of his claims, he tried to force his way in. He was rewarded by a policeman, who grabbed him by the scruff of his neck and, with one giant shove, pushed him all the way down the stairs, almost breaking his neck and right leg. I believe that this poor green fellow is sick still, hurting badly even today.

A writer, describing this incident in the periodical *The S*——, observed:

> I honestly don't know how properly to describe Orthodox Judaism here in New York. Will one of our dear brethren downtown kindly explain what is meant by age-old Judaism? What do they mean when they talk of Torah, religion, and tradition, to which all fervently wish to hold fast? I, to my great sorrow, did not grow up among learned people, and never studied enough to understand the various prohibitions, fences, and self-imposed restraints that are found in the vineyard of our holy religion. But I do know this: carrying and business are among the two most stringent Sabbath prohibitions. The *Shulchan Aruch,* the lifeblood of true Judaism, includes long chapters on these matters. The rabbis of blessed memory annulled the blowing of the shofar, taking up of the *lulav,* and many other great and important commandments when holidays fell on the Sabbath on the basis of the principle: "lest you take it up and carry it four cubits within the public domain" [Sukah 43a]. They also always took great pains in the matter of the *eruv* [the symbolic intermingling of domains, which permit Jews to carry things on the Sabbath]. Amble round the cities of

Europe and see for yourselves. But you are not careful at
all. Old, venerable Orthodox Jews walk in the streets carrying in their hands their prayer shawls and prayerbooks
without any hint of shame. Some even take along walking
sticks and other objects. Have you now made this a positive
commandment? It seems as if you are afraid that many still
value themselves and do not want to learn your ways, so you
try to impose them by force: closing the doors of the
sanctuary before all who refuse to follow you in public
violation of the Sabbath. Many of us are also aware of the
hidden fact that there is no danger to those who, because of
forgetfulness or business engagements, are unable to secure
advanced tickets on Friday. It is possible to secure a ticket
even on the Sabbath while prayers are going on. I have seen
with my own eyes the vast business carried out at the door
by trustees, aided by policemen. Is it not a criminal offense?
Have such things ever been known in Israel? Is this Orthodox Judaism? Even besides the prohibition, is the synagogue a playhouse? Is it a dance hall or a game room that
requires guarding? Why do you steal from the poor? You
might have earned forgiveness for your *chazanim* and your
multicolored synagogues, but how do you slam the door
before one who comes to pour out his heart before the
Almighty?

The honorable author continued in this vein to ask question after
question. He then proceeded to pit American communities and the holy
communities of Europe, one against the other. His conclusions were
unanswerable and altogether correct—but for the moment we forbear
copying them: the proper time has not yet come.

    This writer, who I believe was born in Holland, has never had the
opportunity to study Jewish texts or learn under scholars. What he knows
about Judaism derives, by his own admission, only from what he has
heard or experienced.

    Now those of you who were born in Hungary and Poland, how do
you respond to that?[25]

    New *chazanim* who succeed in the job market comport themselves
with the greatest majesty and splendor. Our people distribute money to
them as if it grew on trees. Multitudes who for lack of money can't hear
them at least want to view them: the sight of their glorious visages fills
them with happiness.

Fierce winds and terrible storms—arguments, disputes, and debates—carry on at meetings between different factions every time they observe yet another new face and cantorial style. But the *chazanim* themselves are joyful. They feel regret only over times past in their native lands. The lot that has fallen to them here pleases and satisfies them. They are, however, grievously mistaken. They fail to recognize that in the future—soon—they too will fall from favor. And others will come to replace them.

We are unable at this time to describe everything exactly in the full detail it deserves. To do so would require our devoting to this subject an entire book. We leave, therefore, a great deal for our successors to do. May they come and expand on our words.

In former days, even three or four years ago, most New York congregations contented themselves with simple synagogue readers (*baale tefilah*) who were always selected from among those in their own midst. Sabbath prayers never extended longer than two and one half hours. By ten o'clock (or during the next hour, all according to the prevailing custom), we could already see masses of our brethren clustering together in every nook and cranny. Those few who took an interest in Torah could spend a free hour luxuriating in study—something they much regretted being unable to do during the week because of overwork. Those who preferred to delight their souls with music could trudge down to the large synagogues in older and richer communities. These were wise enough back then to recognize the value of music in a house of God. But even they didn't go after the "great and wonderful" and certainly didn't claim exclusive, monopoly rights over their *chazan*. They didn't turn their synagogues into businesses, didn't turn the world upside-down, spending days and years searching, and didn't expend more than they could afford. They, rather, made their selections from among those readily available in the city for a small sum, never exceeding—not even in a single congregation—anything more than $700 annually.

On the one hand, those were good days: congregations didn't have to burden themselves with debts in order to survive, and didn't have to tax their members unbearably. On the other hand, the days were bad indeed: congregations had nothing of importance with which to busy themselves. During synagogue [services], in community halls, and at meetings, arguments and conversation dwelt only on minor matters, small things that recurred over and over without ever changing their form. Had it not been for a few select people with special skills—pure-

hearted, all-wise *luftmenschen,* building castles in the air, always inventing
great and important matters in need of solution—then many a time there
would have been nothing about which to meet, consult, and debate.

In European Hebrew periodicals we often read announcements
about innovative activities and actions undertaken by New York Jewish
congregations. Reporters expound on them at length and judge them,
depending on the subject, as either good or evil. But how wrong they
sometimes are! They do not realize that these things were generally
created on the spur of the moment. Even those that came to fruition
never ripened and developed; they existed only in the mouths of founders
and their lackeys. Here we have already forgotten all about them, for in
the interval entirely new worlds and creations have come into being.
Soon they too will return to the earth from whence they came; nobody
will recall them, either.

So we make a general announcement to all Hebrew publishers in
Europe: don't accept news from here while it is still "hot." Wait a while—
two weeks, four weeks—in the end nothing will be left for you to report.
At least you will then be able to describe things as they are. How we
laughed when we read a few months ago in those two honorable
periodicals *Hamelits* and *Hatsefirah* about some major endeavor here,
undertaken amidst great ceremony, and described in glowing colors, as a
lesson to our brethren in Russia and Poland that they might follow in
America's path. [The reference is probably to the founding of the Jewish
Theological Seminary on January 2, 1887.] What they did not know is
that the entire matter is nothing but imagination, exaggeration, and
deception. The tales they tell describing New York as a city of beauty are
all in vain. This entire thing neither was nor will be. And even if it should
somehow rise and establish itself on one foot, it will never be of any value
to the Jewish people.[26]

Several congregations here, not blessed with wise or spirited men,
have begun to consider a new idea: abandon the incessant meetings and
congregational gatherings and hand leadership over, as customary in
other countries, to assistants and communal leaders. We know many
people here who once were prime movers in the community, standing in
the front ranks of those who oversaw New York communal affairs, but
who now after many years of arduous labor live all alone, far from the
cries of the crowd. Others, equally well known—excellent diplomats who
established congregations, destroyed them, and then made new ones in
their place, always distinguishing themselves for their wisdom and

bravery—admitted to us that if they did not constantly hope for a job
with power and influence, which in their desperate position they badly
need, they too would long ago have left the field, abandoning community work completely. They don't find the same meaning in communal work as once they did. They look now with a certain contentment
upon what goes on around them but see it all as lifeless. Man has no
interest in things that never change. His basic nature calls on him to
innovate.

So times have changed. You have already seen above, dear reader,
that our brethren here have found a new matter with which to concern
themselves—a valuable and weighty matter which, like some natural
spring, will never run dry. It constantly serves up new material, which
must be amassed and developed, providing plenty of work for years to
come.

This powerful movement—the lust for great *chazanim* and larger,
more magnificent synagogues reaching up even unto the heavens—took
hold suddenly among congregations and societies and has in recent days
developed in the most awesome fashion. It has led to a great deal of evil
and taken our people ten steps backward. A few years ago when the great
number of glaring deficiencies in this city's Jewish community used to
arouse us, we would always tell ourselves that "it is still early, better days
are on the way. Congregations are still poor and small, many [members]
have just arrived. We cannot expect the same excellent arrangements
from them that we were used to seeing in our old homelands. As for the
old, rich congregations, likely they also have not yet disposed of many
internal matters. Perhaps they are now preparing themselves to undertake great and wonderful things, hoping eventually to expand their
activities to exceed even those of European communities."

We always looked hopefully toward the three great congregations in
this city. We won't mention their names—it's enough to tell you, beloved
reader, that they are the three oldest, richest, and most significant ones.
They have had large synagogue buildings for twenty years or more, and
they have in addition *batei midrash* filled with many different books. Their
members are mostly wealthy, God-fearing Jews who everywhere proudly
profess their devotion to Orthodox Judaism. Many among them are wise
and Jewishly knowledgeable; they know the Torah, which giants of Israel
taught them in their youth. We expected them at every minute to take the
first step, to lay a cornerstone. What is the cornerstone to building
Judaism? Houses of study to teach Torah and offer rabbinical certification, schools, elementary teachers, heads of *yeshivot,* and Jewish courts.

We were, however, very much mistaken. Half our prophecy did in fact come true, as these congregations became the first to awaken from their slumber and institute far-reaching changes. But the changes were hardly those that we had dreamed about and awaited impatiently. They were, rather, those we have already mentioned: nice, attractive, and of considerable benefit to some people. Who can deny that a sweet-singing *chazan* is pleasing to the ear? Who won't admit that a magnificent, large, and spacious synagogue is more pleasant than a small and narrow *bes midrash*? Some even went further, beyond the strict letter of the law, and brought not only *chazanim* in the sense of sweet-singing cantors, but actually wonderful artistic experts, sublime singers, men so heavily imbued with musical wisdom that they could earn a leisurely living even without a synagogue, just from their magnificent talent. Nor did they stop at expanding the synagogue or even, as many smaller congregations did, at increasing its splendor. Instead, they completely destroyed the old structure, leaving not even a trace, or they sold out to others for a low price and built in their stead beautiful "houses of God," the likes of which have never been seen in the Orthodox community. Whosoever enters feels as though he has entered Paradise itself (see Author's Note D). It seems to us that the three synagogues cost about $250,000, and their expenses last year came in each place to between $12,000 and $15,000, almost $50,000 all together. Have you ever heard of such a thing in all your life? Fifty thousand dollars! All from three congregations that all together don't have more than 300 members. And don't forget, beloved reader, that no chief justice [*av bes din*], *shochet,* judge, *batlan,* student, teacher, widow, or orphan has yet benefited from this sum; indeed the sum is lost to charity. Such is the truth; no exaggeration or hyperbole. Proof may be found in the fact that now, in their second year, they have been forced to pass special regulations and level additional taxes and assessments. Now what do you think, dear reader; is this not a wonderful step forward? A vigorous change? But will this change bring any benefit to Judaism in general? Will the innovations be strong enough to return children to their mother's bosom? We doubt it very much, though we hope our prophecy proves incorrect, because these changes neither benefit anyone nor improve anything. They do, however, have within them the power to destroy completely "the saving remnant"—that small but good portion that God in His mercy has left us. They can shut off the path of light, blocking its access to this city and land forever.

11 Solutions

Recently one of the honorable writers who involves himself a great deal in communal affairs roused himself to publish, at his own expense, an open letter addressed to all Orthodox societies and congregations calling on them to congress together for at least one month in order to decide how to prevent defections, repair misdeeds, and stop the terrible evil that looms ominously over the face of Judaism in this country. The honorable author was not content just to offer good advice. He attempted to put his own words into practice. He established a committee, set a time and a place, and called on every group and congregation, as well as on every man who had the fear of God in his heart, to send their names in writing to him or to one of the other general overseers. He urged them to act quickly, for great and wonderful things were to be accomplished. To his mind this was the only way to bring about his aims: to breath life into dry bones [see Ezekiel 37], to unite the various parties of Israel, and to raise in our midst the beacon of religion and Torah that has grown exceedingly faint.

This is what our fathers always did whenever they saw Judaism confronted by danger. In all other countries Jews do this even today; indeed, it is only by force of these great, general congresses that evils have been stymied and obstacles removed from Israel's path. So the aims are desirable—we know that the author truly hopes to be helpful and to make improvements. It would seem appropriate for us to extend to him our approbation for his courage and bravery. But he exceeded his bounds. In his innocence or haste he forgot that he is a mere writer, not the head of a *kolel* [an advanced talmudic academy] or the rabbi of his people. A writer is entitled to reprove, moralize, teach, opine, advise, scheme, and indeed to write anything that he pleases for the benefit of his people and their faith. But act he may not do. He may not assume undertakings appropriate to notables and giants of the faith. Therefore, instead of furthering and facilitating the cause to which he is so devoted, he has in fact injured it considerably. Many are now found calling after him: "Who made you chief and ruler over us?" [Exodus 2:14]. "Are you our equal?" (cf. Psalm 55:14). Indeed what our dear writer has arrogated to himself is no small thing! His thinking is correct, and he is an excellent member of the community, but advantageous as this is, it does not qualify him to call general meetings together and undertake on his own a matter affecting thousands of Jews—especially not in America where the number of *parnasim,* leaders, directors, chiefs, and representatives is so great. Every congregation, after all, has at least one well-known person of competence. Not only will such people not lend a hand, much less participate in any activities; they will actually band together in opposition, invalidate the gathering, and place obstacles all over its path.

We might even have forgiven the writer this, for his aim was laudable, and he surely wished personally to uphold the rabbinic dictim: "In a place where there are no men, strive to be a man" [Avot 2:6]. What we cannot forgive are the errors and lack of expertise he displayed in the matter with which he is centrally concerned. We are astonished at this writer: he did not arrive here yesterday, and has surely seen and heard a great deal, perhaps more than we have. He had time to learn that this kind of meeting can bring about no benefit. All it can do is give the masses something new with which to occupy themselves. The cause is a good one for idlers who despise their work. It will provide raw material for many an argument and sermon.

The case for a congress based on congresses of previous generations and those of our own day in other countries is in a sense completely true. We too know of the benefits that these conferences brought to Israel. But how things have changed from then until now, and from there to here! How could a writer so mistakenly associate the one with the other when they have nothing in common? Those who met to fortify the wall of faith, whether in the past or in the present, all were true to the faith of Israel. They were great men, excelling in wisdom, righteousness, and piety; men whose thoughts, desires, and wishes completely centered around their people; men who cast aside all their personal worries and needs, devoting their physical and spiritual energies entirely to their religion and faith. Yet even they did not trust themselves; in everything they would first ask the opinion of their great teachers, the famous *gaonim* who brightened the land with their Torah and holiness. In turn, they would in most cases take part in the congresses, spreading upon them the spirit of their wisdom and guiding them with their advice. These great men did not content themselves with small talk, sermons, and pleasant conversation, and did not assume that by their plaudits alone they had seized the fat from the fire. They rather fought like true heroes, refusing to leave the fray, rest, or keep silent until they had carried their plans into effect, set up necessary restrictions, and repaired the breaches in Israel's surrounding wall. Frequently aid came to them from governments or officials—when holy *gaonim* agreed to grovel at their feet, entreating them to provide help so as not to lose the lingering remnant of their dear subjects. These saintly officials—their majestic splendor similar to that of the Almighty Himself, their actions holy, their motives pure, their wisdom Divine—performed as their heart and spirit dictated. They approved all the [congress's] decrees, endowed them with the force of law, and in this way gave them currency among the nation.

How different will this forthcoming congress be! How many thousands of contrasts distinguish the kind of holy, scholarly convocation of Jewish leaders that we have discussed from the American congress that this author dreams about! Assume he finds no obstacles in his path, and all the leaders of Israel in this city and in other regions and cities of the nation—plus important and famous notables, like manufacturers, pawnbrokers, jewelers, stockholders, and storekeepers, as well as master peddlers, tailors, shoemakers, and tanners, and even *magidim,* preachers, reverends, *chazanim, mohalim,* marriage officiators, and all other notables from organizations, associations, lodges, and societies—all gathered together as per his order. Assume they had already convened at a single vast meeting and had sat together for a full month, nights included, just as the author and proponent of this grand idea wants. Then assume that they had already written changes, promulgated edicts, and instituted restrictions. Now the congress has finished its work, and the delegates have returned home in full accord. All restrictions and preventive measures have been willingly and lovingly accepted—everything is done. Tell us, dear author, what would happen next? Who would carry into effect the thoughts of these good men? How would the decrees and regulations move from theory to practice? Who would carry them out? Who would give them currency in Israel?

The chairman of the congress? He is, without doubt, one of the leading and most venerable of the *parnasim,* an active worker in various organizations who did not hesitate to display his power in the great and holy assembly that already took place here. But yesterday's actions are to him only a memory. Today he stands up to his neck in business and leisure activities. Just as he enjoyed the congress for a month, now he has found other things to play with. In New York there is something new every morning for those with ability and wealth.

What of the vice chairman, his assistant, and all the other leaders and spokesmen? They too have returned to their own work. Far be it from us to cast aspersions: they are certainly busy and could not possibly devote days on end to communal matters. The three days of the [already convened, preliminary] conference were enough to show their love and regard for their religion; they did not sleep a wink until all the delegates had signed and accepted the new arrangements. But never did they personally intend to stick out their necks by becoming implementers. They don't even need these things: their sons have already graduated from college and become refined; their daughters have already learned to dance, sing, and read novels. They are grown up; they will not go back to seek instruction from Russian and Polish teachers in Jewish schools. Nor, if they have become devoted to reforms, will they change their home lives and become more scrupulous. What then can these enlightened Yankees say? So many of the things they are dealing with are strange to them. The subject must therefore be left to the preachers who have the time, the desire, and the capability to accept these regulations upon themselves, thereby setting an example for others to follow. If this is the case, though, how will the regulations of such wise laymen help us? What do we need a congress for? Are New York preachers short of things to say? Have they run out of material for sermons? What news can they tell the nation that it has not already heard from the [first] meeting and from the [local] Jewish Supreme Court [the *Bes Din Hagadol*]? Why all this bother?

In short the writer made an error. Fortunately he dropped his idea, and did not create a worldwide sensation about something that would have had no value. Had his wish been translated into action, the truth of our words would have been proved: he was the wrong man at the wrong time to bring the idea to fruition. New York gatherings—the kind that he wanted—are all alike. Only a change in name separates a simple meeting from a great congress. Both combined cannot succeed in bringing about the goal that we seek: to raise the glory of religion and Torah in this city and land.

I am surprised, dear writer, at how quickly you have forgotten the great commotion stirred up for two full years by a group calling itself the U.H.O.A.[27] It too had been established to repair breaches that had developed in the walls of our religion. It met from time to time, and periodically sent out announcements, letters, reprimands, and open warnings. It called on congregations, societies, and on all sections of the nation to gather and participate in its lofty activities. Occasionally, in journals and open letters, it boasted that it had succeeded in removing many obstacles and corruptions, and held high hopes of scaling the mountain altogether and accomplishing many more great things for Israel. Authors and writers became ecstatic. Young people brought joy to distant acquaintances with the wonderfully comforting news that even in America the Torah had found its redeemers, and Jews were beginning to ready themselves for divine work. One of the journals here extolled its virtues ceaselessly and regularly filled two to three pages with articles detailing its activities. But while others busied themselves tooting its horn and shouting its praises to heaven, it had already shut its eyes and passed away, leaving after it nothing to show for all its wondrous activities.

A year and a half ago, when the society still existed, a loved one of mine in the city of Chicago asked me in a letter my opinion of it. I replied as follows:

> You rejoice in vain, my friend, and similarly in vain were the efforts of a poet in your city who authored a rhymed verse in classical meter extolling this organization's activities, for it has no power to do any good at all for Judaism. It accomplishes nothing, though I read a great deal of sound and fury about it. What was will continue to be; what wasn't won't be. Nothing it will do, I am sorry to say, will change matters even slightly from the way they are now. There are several reasons for this which I cannot completely spell out in this letter, but let me mention several of them, and from these you should be able to work out the rest.
>
> 1. The members of this society are all men engaged in wordly affairs: merchants, peddlers, and laborers who are physically and monetarily absorbed in their jobs. I don't know of even one of them who would be free of work, anxiety and doubt, and therefore able to devote all his

strength and time to the good of the society and its lofty
aims. A broad society like this one, which deals with the
needs of the entire nation, requires at least ten notable
people who are free from work and have no concerns in the
world save that to which they have decided to devote their
attention.

2. The spokesmen, directors, and leaders chosen to
guide the activities and affairs of the society, while important
and respected in their communities, are not outstanding
enough to draw public opinion around them, to make tens
of thousands of Jews act according to their will. Their words
and speeches are all fine and well when delivered from the
podium, proclaiming the purpose of gathering and putting
the meeting in proper perspective. But they lack the necessary power to penetrate deeply into the hearts of the people,
to give them currency among the nation as a whole.

3. Lengthy sermons, printed warnings and rebukes in
periodicals, and open letters—the principal results of their
activities up to now—are not the most effective means of
changing people's ways. As preachers increase in number,
their words lose their power. Printed warnings are even
worse! American Jews are fed up with *kashrus* proclama-
tions. They make no impact upon them whatsoever.

4. Those who aim to change the world, who stand on a
pedestal and preach Torah and morals to the public must
not only practice what they preach. They must also be
people who separate themselves from the rest of the nation
in every way, making their every action superior. Sadly, we
see that many of the great activists here—those with ener-
getic tongues who are the leading speakers at any meeting—
not only fail to demonstrate "extra piety," but actually do
the reverse of what they ask of others. They scream, for
example, about the degenerate state of education and the
terrible tragedy that looms over Judaism from this younger
generation. Yet not one of their own children or grandchildren has ever seen a Hebrew Bible, much less a Gemara,
though these are men of means who have no need to wait
until improvements, like a communal *bes midrash*, are
effected. They scream about the disorderly state of *kashrus* in
general. Yet it never occcurs to them to ask their wives where
they purchase their meat, or for that matter their milk, and
certainly not anything else. They scream that the dignity of
Torah is at a low ebb, and that scholars no longer receive

respect. But to whom do they give their respect—and their daughters' hands in marriage: to pious scholars or to lawyers and doctors?

Now, my friend, decide for yourself: Can we hope for much from these "generals"? In forthcoming letters I'll tell you other things that I have held back today, and you'll see that neither laziness nor arrogance has prevented me from joining this society, something which you have expressed amazement about many times. It is, rather, that I wish not to be false either to myself or to others—but enough for now.[28]

Despite all of these things, we have neither despaired nor given up hope. We trust that our faith in the eternality of Israel and its Torah will never leave us, and that even here the condition of Judaism will change for the better. We trust that our brethren will yet awaken from their slumbers and see how far they have strayed from the true path of Orthodox Judaism. May their eyes be opened to see the terrible tragedy that looms over our Torah and religion if things remain much longer as they are now. May they see the moral rot that pervades the youth who must carry the banner of Judaism forward. May their hearts and memories be stirred to the realization that the hour for action has arrived. Heal the breach while there is still time, while the house still stands, before it is utterly destroyed.

"What can be done?" readers will justifiably ask. "How can we escape destruction?" A great and important question! Our brethren must become conscious of their disease and try to improve their condition. Many solutions can still be found.

We shall devote an entire volume, Part Two of this book, to solving this conundrum. There, dear readers, we shall tell you those things that, in our view, may properly bring us toward our goal: to accelerate the future development of our pure faith, and to create a truly enduring basis for the building of Judaism in this city. But since we don't know if we shall soon succeed in carrying out our plan to print part two, we herewith present in our concluding remarks a few of our ideas. We trust that our readers will comprehend their truth, though we cannot now explain our aim in precise detail.

1. Unification. Form one large congregation and society for every twenty small ones that now bring no benefit to either Israel or its Torah. In New York we should not have more than ten or twelve different congregations.

2. Association. The twelve separate congregations should work together and unite into one central power for all matters that relate to the community as a whole.

3. Establish rabbis. This requires no explanation. We mean, obviously, that God's people should not be like sheep without a shepherd—as they are today. Rather, each congregation should establish at its head a man of stature and greatness in Torah, wisdom, and piety to guide them, instruct them, and tell them how to act.

4. Create a chief rabbinate or [overall] Jewish Supreme Court, and raise the dignity of and concern with Torah, its investigation, and its study. This requires a lengthy exposition, which cannot be summarized here. All will be explained in the appropriate place.

These are the major points that we have in mind to discuss. We have already dealt with them somewhat in an article that we published last year. But we did not then explain things properly. We neither disclosed the means of securing our aims nor detailed their redeeming qualities. Our words, therefore, had no benefit; God willing, we shall make everything clear in the future.

We leave our readers with this prayer: May God have mercy on the remnant of Israel, and fulfill in our day what was written by his servants and prophets: "At that time I will gather you, and at [that] time I will bring you [home]. For I will make you renowned and famous among all the peoples of the earth when I restore your fortunes before their very eyes. And this shall be my covenant with them, said the Lord. My spirit which is upon you, and the words which I have placed in your mouth shall not depart from your mouth, nor from the mouth of your children, nor from the mouth of your children's children—said the Lord—from now on, for all time" [Zephaniah 3:20; Isaiah 59:21].

Appendix: A Letter of Friendship

To my honorable friend, the beloved, brilliant, and dear rabbi, preeminent among eminent scholars, enormously learned, sharp-witted, and fully pious, whose revered name is his glory, our master, Rabbi Z——, in the city of K—— in Hungary, may his light shine forth.

Your dear letter, which like its predecessors is filled to the brim with various questions about this city and its Jewish affairs, has reached me. I hasten to carry out your request in part, although at this time I am pressed from all sides, and it seems to me that I have fulfilled my obligation to you in my previous letters where I expanded at even greater length than I was allotted. Still, because of my great love toward you, your wisdom, your Torah, and your goodheartedness, I once again cannot refuse you. I shall endeavor to answer some of your questions.

Congregation Beth Hamedrash Hagodol in this city, which your friend, our master Rabbi M—— from the village of R—— told you many pleasant things about, is not the same as the Hungarian Congregation Beth Hamedrash Hagodol, which is not yet four years old and which I told you about in my earlier letter. When your aforementioned friend lived here, it did not even exist. Both places, however, are goodly and pleasant; both are known and praised. The difference between them is that the first congregation is old and wealthy, its *bes hamidrash* is large and ample—five hundred students could find a place there—its synagogue is a huge, magnificent building, one of the grandest and finest synagogues in the city, and most of its members are prosperous, powerful, and prominent. Even those there who study and know Torah are great merchants, men of substance and wealth. This honorable congregation could work wonders at raising the honor and dignity of Torah.

The second congregation, however, is poor and young. All its money and resources together do not exceed $3,000. Its *bes hamidrash* is small and narrow (the leaders of the congregation are now trying to establish a large, beautiful, and amply wide *bes hamidrash*: may God come to their aid[29]), and cannot hold even 150 men. Its members are mostly all people who support themselves with difficulty by the work of their own hands: the number of wealthy people or businessmen among them is small. The founders called it "the Great Synagogue" [*hagodol*] because of the holy and lofty purpose that it set for itself: "to raise the honor and majesty of the Torah." Although things have not gone exactly as the founders wanted, we cannot deprive the congregation of its honorable name, for most of its members are acquainted with God's Torah and are familiar with Jewish books, and many are excellent scholars who set special times aside for Torah study. This, to be sure, is not a rare phenomenon in this city. Among our Russian and Polish brothers we see this in almost every large congregation, especially in the Beth Hamedrash Hagodol mentioned above. We hear that even uptown [on 54th Street] there is a congregation named Orach Chayim, whose members are enormously wealthy and completely German—that is from Germany and Prussia—and who gather daily after the afternoon prayers [*minchah*] to enjoy Torah study. But this congregation, the Hungarian Congregation Beth Hamedrash Hagodol, distinguishes itself by what people study together. They learn as a congregation, and in smaller groups: pilpulistically [the dialectical method], deliberately, and sharply. At various times, especially on *Shabas Shuvah* and *Shabas Hagadol* [the Sabbaths before Yom Kippur and Passover], they study a special section of talmudic law which outstanding members expound publicly—a phenomenon not frequently found in this city and land. But will their children follow in their ways? Will they enjoy, as their fathers did, God's holy Torah and the wisdom of our holy rabbis of blessed memory? I doubt it very much; at this time we have no hope at all. Only time will tell.

The honorable *Ahavas Tsiyon* [Love of Zion] Society of Hungarian immigrants aims to support those from our country now sitting before God in Jerusalem and other holy cities. It was founded seven years ago by a person from our homeland who was sent by the leaders of *Kolel Shomrei Chomos* (Guardian of the Walls Advanced Talmud Academy): the brilliant, dear rabbi, whose ideas are pure, whose intelligence is sharp, and who is full of lofty, honorable virtues, his revered name is his glory, our master, Rabbi Jehoshua Stampfer [1852-1908], may his light shine forth. All the glory of this dear man—his virtues, his contributions and his principles—I'll write to you about at some other time. Some twenty years ago he left our country [Hungary], and until three years ago he lived in Jerusalem. Now he lives on his own plot in the colony of Petach Tikva [which he founded].

The honorable *Chovevei Tsiyon* [Lovers of Zion] Society of Russian and Polish immigrants was founded three or four years ago and aims both to support our colonist brethren who are working the holy soil and to further the idea of Eretz Israel settlement in general. Society members are in the main upstanding men of knowledge, many of them are scholars, intellectuals, and excellent writers. They aim with all their might to raise the dignity of their society and to increase its membership in cities across the country. I regret to say, however, that this society, which includes some 400 members, has not a single person from among our Hungarian countrymen.

With regard to *mikva'os* [ritual baths]—the means of constructing them and keeping them kosher—it is very difficult, for we have neither wells nor running streams. All the water comes through pipes and it must be rendered kosher through snow, ice, and rainwater. I have already written to the *gaon*, the head of the *bes din*, and asked him to give you my letter where I have properly explained everything. You will see there that, in this great matter as well, we must rely on the evidence and trustworthiness of one person: the bath attendant. In New York the bath attendants are not all righteous people. Moreover, there are days when it is impossible to rely even on the righteous and innocent among them, for example before the holidays—especially the high holidays—when their burdens and work are great. But who will pay heed to such things? The few poor rabbis whom we have here make the *mikvah* kosher initially, and get paid. After they have certified it, they have nothing more to do with it: possession passes to the hands of the bath attendant. The masses, involved up to their necks in the quest for food and money, know nothing about the new halachic requirements in America, which demand that they be scrupulously careful even about bath attendants. The obstacles in this matter are great.

May the honorable society *Anshei Sfarad* (our countrymen) be remembered favorably for having made a great improvement in this situation. The *mikvah* that it established last year under their *bes hamidrash* was made in the best fashion: two trenches one next to the other, with a dividing wall between them that is breached at the top in such a way that when one side is filled, the other fills up through the breach. This prevents falling into error, as is explained completely in the responsum of [Moses Sofer], the *Chosom Sofer* [see Yoreh De'ah responsum 203].

With regard to Sabbath observance—the stopping of manual labor and other work in factories, stores, and businesses—hundreds and even thousands of people are careful. In many New York streets and markets you won't find even one open store. The Sabbath tranquility compares favorably to that found in most Jewish areas. On the other hand, there is a great deal of laxity with regard to the Sabbath prohibitions against carrying, handling forbidden items, and doing indirect business. Even Jews who otherwise act entirely properly do not hesitate to be lenient in these actions—brazenly and in public. And yet they are good Orthodox Jews nonetheless.

With regard to the *mitsvah* of Sukos [Tabernacles], people are now far more scrupulous than in previous years. When I arrived here, I found not more than one or two *sukos* in the entire region where I reside. Now, just on the street where I have my business, there are more than twenty—though most people fulfill their obligation simply by making *kidush* [they make a blessing over the wine in the *sukah*] and then return home for the full meal. Some do this from fear of unruly children, Jews among them, who are found, sad to say, in every building and throw stones. Others just take the *mitsvah* of Sukos lightly and therefore perform it indoors.

The commentary volume of novellae on Tractate *Yevamos* that you saw in my house ten years ago, where there were copied the teachings of our rabbi and truly lofty *gaon*, light of the exile, whose holy and revered name is his glory, our master, Rabbi Meir Perles [1811–93], may his light shine forth, head of the *bes din* and communal rabbi of the holy congregation in Caroli [Carei=Mare], was unfortunately lost by me in the course of time. I cannot therefore fulfill your request. To turn directly to this holy rabbi and *gaon*, may his light shine forth, will also be of no help, for I am familiar with his holy ways: he writes nothing down in books and answers but one out of a thousand halachic questions put to him. I recall our once asking him about this during our yeshiva studies. He answered us first in jest: [I forbear for fear of] dropsy, which is a sign [of sin (Shabat 33a)]. Later he turned to us and in a charming voice said, "Know, my dear ones, that I have a great deal of my own work to accomplish. Rather than becoming a teacher of many great and excellent people who have no need of me, I am better off dedicating my time to youths like yourselves who do need a teacher like me."

And that's just what he did. He dedicated his entire life and time to students, whom he loved with all his heart and soul. He never monitored whether the older, more experienced students gathered [to study]. They often stopped coming entirely, not having the time for three separate classes. Our rabbi wasn't sorry at all. Happy as he was to climb mountains with his sharp dialectics—and he would clamber up and down, penetrating to the depths and clarifying every word completely, encouraged by the sight of an understanding student in front of him—so he was happy and joyful when studying with little children a page of Gemara according to the simple meaning of the text. He would turn it around and review it before them several times over, until he saw that they knew their studies fluently. He comported with them exactly like a teacher of primary school.

His own work, his industry, his wonderful perseverance in God's Torah is truly beyond measure and worth, almost above human nature. It can really be said about him that from the day he matured, he never stopped his incessant studying. Nor was he satisfied merely to search and investigate; rather, he toiled at his studies endlessly with all his strength. He weighed his every word, and not one—not even a single letter—passed over his lips until he had scrutinized it thoroughly and pronounced it meticulously. So it was with the words of the Gemara, the commentators, and everything else that he learned or took a fancy to, for he laid great stress on "the law of enlightening letters" [the value of the written word]. He thus did not skip around while studying; he did not move from subject to subject as was customary in almost all *yeshivos* of our country [Hungary]. He rather followed a fixed order in all his studies. He passed over nothing as too simple. Indeed, on Shabas Hagadol and Shabas Shuvah [the Sabbaths before Passover and the Day of Atonement], he sometimes extracted [as his text] laws from places that not one of the commentators had written anything about because of their seeming simplicity. We students did not conceal from our rabbi that we knew not what these could teach us. He then built upon them [homiletical] towers, wonderfully fantastic [scholarly] constructs worthy of a [Lithuanian talmudist like Ayreh Leib Gunzberg, author of the] *Sha'agas Aryeh* [1755] or [a Prague talmudist like Jonathan Eybeschuetz, author of the commentary on the *Choshen Mishpat* entitled] *The Tumim* (1775–77). Still, homiletics were never of central importance to him. He always warned us not to spend our time on dialectics [*pilpulim*], for they are in no way useful. He only engaged in them himself for mental stimulation.

At times we spoke with him about the great figures of the past. He always had a mine of information about these very brilliant scholars who were so dear to him. His style and manner of teaching bore witness to this, as all the students knew. More than once we found our holy rabbi (may he live a long life) standing and studying with all his might, as was his wont, those places in the Talmud that almost every schoolboy knows fluently. He would review them and repeat them over and over without taking any commentary into his hand, and without any seeming desire to study the subject in depth in order to say something new about it. He rather wanted to remember what he had learned, so that it would be incised into his brain, never to be forgotten. We never ceased to be amazed: a man about whom it could be said—as it was said of the brilliant author of the *Sha'agas Aryeh*—that he could recite the essence of the Talmud and its commentaries in a single hour; a man who already forty-five years earlier was known as a great *gaon*; a man whose wisdom, greatness, diligence, and ability to sit all day learning with small children uninitiated into legal style astounded all the great men of Israel; a man unfazed by any secrets, and expert in all areas of Torah and wisdom; a man who toppled mountains and ground them together during the course of his investigations; a man whose every word was a completed book and who could, with a slight motion, invalidate everything new that a veteran student might ever say; a man who could stand for hours over a simple subject, constantly reviewing it without ever becoming tired or weary, but seeing it with fresh eyes each time—such a remarkable man is our rabbi and *gaon*, may his light shine forth. We do not have many Meir Perleses in our generation.

But sad to say, and sadly for all Israel, this veritable Torah scroll has passed all his life in sorrow. I personally have seen his grief and bitterness—it is the cause of our rabbi's refusal to intervene in the affairs of Israel, and of all the other things that we spoke about in earlier letters. God willing, I shall speak more to you about this.[30]

I received the valuable book *Chasan Sofer*, parts one and two, by our master, teacher and rabbi, the righteous and holy *gaon*, as pure as an angel of God, whose holy and revered name is his glory, our master, Rabbi Samuel Ehrenfeld [1835–83], of blessed memory, from his own holy hand. He sent the volumes to me, with love and affection, where I used to live, in the city of Kniesen in the province of Zips [=Szepes]. I used then to dispatch letters and questions to him from time to time, and his honorable esteemed holiness always answered me with great humility and righteousness. His love for his students, even the youngest among them, was unbounded: he looked upon all of them as his own sons. Then it fell to my lot, along with my entire family, to leave my country and homeland. Since coming to this country—[a wilderness] neither seeded nor watered—the ties binding me to my revered and brilliant masters were broken. I heard from them only infrequently.

When I had the chance some years ago to establish a house of Torah among our countrymen here, it occurred to me to inform my honorable and righteous teacher, for I knew that he would remember me and be gladdened by my news. It came then as a sudden arrow, a thunderbolt that shook and laid waste our hearts, when we heard the sudden, bitter news that God had taken our *gaon*, the rabbi, and he was no more. I was shocked. I could not stop crying and yelling bitterly about my loss and that of all Israel. For many days I hardly knew myself. As I recovered a bit, I called our countrymen together to wail and mourn at our Beth Hamedrash Hagodol. I eulogized our rabbi (may the memory of the righteous be for a blessing) as a student faithfully devoted to him with all my heart and soul. Those gathered, including elders and scholars, all cried bitterly. Tears poured like water from all my listeners as I painted the terrible picture of the great loss that our generation had suffered in the fire that God had set in the house of Israel.

If I did not consider myself unworthy, I would print the entire eulogy, which I have preserved in manuscript. In it, students and admirers of our brilliant rabbi (may the memory of the righteous be for a blessing) would discover many things that they knew nothing about, for I was privileged to serve beside him above the rest of the students, even those greater and better than I. I was privileged to be able to copy his novellae and to organize his sermons. For three years I came to his house daily, and witnessed all his holy ways. But I know that no eulogy written by one who like myself lives in America can have any substance to it: nobody would read it. So I forbear printing it.

The good news that our master, teacher, and rabbi, the excellent *gaon* and wise man of the community, may his name be glorious and holy, our master, Rabbi Eleazer Loew [1839–1917], may his light shine forth, was appointed to head the *bes din* of Ungvár [Uzhgorod], arrived here several weeks ago in the journal [*Neue Pester Zeitung*(?)] and we were pleased. Still, we are most sorry that matters had reached the point that the *gaon* (may his light shine forth) would leave the city that he had served spiritually for twelve years, having filled the position of his father, the magnificent *gaon* and knight of the Torah, may his name be glorious and holy, our master, Rabbi Jeremiah [Loew, 1811–74]. How long will [the angel of death's] sword continue to cause mourning in our land?

The pleasant news that our master, teacher, and rabbi, the great, famous, and righteous rabbi, whose holy and revered name is his glory, our master Rabbi Moses Sofer [?–1917], may his light shine forth, was appointed head of the *bes din* of Homonna elevated my spirits and brought me satisfaction and pleasure. But it wasn't necessary for you to elaborate the praises of this great rabbi in your letter, for who knows better than I his great and lofty worth, his modesty, uprightness, righteousness, and piety! Know, my dear friend, that I sat at his feet for three years while he still engaged in business. Torah and wealth were united at his table. After my father (may his light shine forth), he was my first instructor in the ways of Torah. His relationship to me was like that of a father to a son. I could tell you far more than you told me in your letter; indeed you do not know even a tenth of his contributions, attributes, and virtues. Glory to the people of Homonna who chose to place him at their head. For this Moses is enormously respected by all the great men of Israel in our country. He will yet increase in splendor and majesty, and many will be drawn to him.

I come now to your words of Torah. Know, my dear friend, that all that you wrote me regarding the transaction of business on holidays is not new to me. I have already seen all the citations that you indicated, except for a few, which I couldn't examine because I do not have the books and they are not found in this city. I am surprised that while you pointed out almost all the citations that are relevant to this subject, you did not mention the original source, which is found in Nahmanides's commentary to the Torah, in the portion of *Emor* [Leviticus 23:24] cited in the *Chosom Sofer* paragraph [responsa] 195 of *Choshen Mishpat*. Nahmanides of blessed memory there says that we are commanded by the Torah to rest on a holiday even from things that are not [officially designated as] work. One should not be engaged all day in wearisome tasks: measuring out crops in the field, weighing up fruits, etc., lest the marketplace fill with all sorts of buying and selling, shops remain open, storekeepers give credit, money-changers sit at their table with gold coins before them, and workers get up to go to work, hiring themselves out as on any weekday. Because of precisely such things, which do not have the [official] character of work, the Torah employed the word *shabason*, that it might be a day of rest—which is a good and beautiful interpretation.

I know not how to judge: have you never seen these words or did you not write them because they are so well known?

Regrettably, everything that Nahmanides of blessed memory portrayed in this comment can now be seen in this large city filled with societies, congregations, *parnasim*, treasurers, *chazanim*, and prayer readers, as well as many Orthodox storekeepers who observe the Sabbath according to the law, but open their stores on the holidays to sell, write, tear, weigh, accept money, and exchange—especially on the second day of the holiday (*yom tov sheni shel galuyos*), when in their eyes trade is absolutely permissible, just as on a weekday. A great many Jewish women here—pious, righteous women, careful to choose a seat near the front of the women's gallery so that they may hear the sounds of joy and prayer; women always intervening in community affairs, like the matter of *matsos* and bakers and that involving meat, slaughterers, and butchers; women whose husbands would not walk a step without asking them and their saying Yes—these righteous women, while their husbands are joyfully sitting before God in the *bes midrash*, acting according to the will of their Creator who gave us holidays to enjoy, are bustling about from store to store, large baskets on their arms, paying full price for all the necessities in honor of that holiday that they had already desecrated twenty times over. Don't think, my friend, that these women are worldly-wise, native-born, or enlightened Prussians and French; they are, rather, those who a year or two ago ate salty fish and stinking lentils in Jászmigrad or Radomyshl, and certainly did not sense any bad odor in day-old meat. They were then not so spoiled that everything had to be new, brought into being that very day, and they didn't handle money on the holidays even with their little pinky. Yes, how awesome is the strength of America! In a single year it transforms "Rachel the wife of Reb Jacob" into "Mrs. Jacobs," and "Reb Baruch the cobbler and shoemaker" into "Mr. Benet Shoe Manufacturer." The Enlightenments of Berlin and Europe put together did not accomplish as much in half a century. A word to the wise is sufficient.

I noticed in the margins of your letter, after you argued learnedly and with tremendous expertise on the subject of the prohibition implied in the words "thou shalt not deviate," that you quoted the words of Maimonides in the *Guide of the Perplexed* to the effect that one is commanded to heed the words of the wise, and not stray from them, even when they are, heaven forbid, opposed to the truth. As soon as I read your words, I hurried to take in hand my *Guide*; I searched through it without being able to find the words that you used. I almost concluded that you had in mind the words that he wrote in his commentary to *The Ethics of the Fathers* [Avot 1:3] regarding a rebellious scholar, and that you had misinterpreted them. Later, however, I found the words, though not quite exactly the way you wrote them, and not in Maimonides but in *Sefer Hachinuch*, with which you accidentally mixed it up. The language was not as abbreviated as yours—stripped of a beginning and end, and designed to shock the reader—I, rather, found the original, full wording. Its warning, its every word and utterance, is truly as clear as day. The author of blessed memory says in the biblical portion of *Mishpatim* [see the edited and translated edition by Charles Wengrov (Jerusalem, 1978) pp. 310ff.] that commandment 78 is to follow the rule of the majority, for the majority of opinions will always recognize the truth more readily than the minority. But whether in the opinion of the hearer they recognize it or not, the law holds that we should not stray from the majority's course. The root of this commandment lies in our obligation to strengthen the observance and fulfillment of our faith, for had we been commanded that each person in Israel should uphold the Torah as he understands it to be true, disaster would have resulted. The Torah would have become like several torahs, each person issuing judgments according to his own personal opinion. But now that we are commanded to accept the view of the scholarly majority, there is one Torah for all of us. This plays a large part in our continued existence; we cannot deviate from its [the majority's] view. In carrying out the majority's commandments, we fulfill God's command. Even if, heaven forbid, that sometimes does not lead us to the truth, the sin falls on its [the scholarly majority's] head. This is what our rabbis of blessed memory said in Talmud Horayos [2a, 4b].

In the portion of *Shoftim*, paragraph 496, [commandment 508] he [the author] of blessed memory writes that we have refrained from disputing the bearers of tradition, may they rest in peace, or to change their words or diverge from their commandments in any aspect of Torah, for about this it is said, "Do not stray from the words which you have been told either to the right or to the left [Deuteronomy 17:11]." The root of this commandment lies in the fact that the views of human beings disagree one with the other, and on many things will never be reconciled. The Master of All (bless Him) knew that if every individual human being was allowed to explain the meaning of Torah writings, each one according to his personal wisdom, each would interpret his own way, and Israel would be filled with disputes regarding the meaning of the commandments, the Torah becoming like several torahs. Therefore, God, Master of all wisdom, closed our Torah-of-truth by commanding us to treat it in accordance with the authentic explanation received by our ancient scholars (may they rest in peace). In every generation we should similarly listen to the available scholars. They are the recipients of those past words, they drank in those books, and toiled arduously night and day to understand those sublime expressions and wondrous ideas. By accepting this we direct ourselves to the true path of Torah knowledge. Regarding the truth and glory of this commandment, our rabbis said [Sifre, Shoftim, 154], "Do not swerve to the right or the left—even if you are told [that left is right and right is left, listen]." That is, even if they [scholars] err on some matter, all should submit to their invariably better view. Each individual should not act according to his personal view, that would lead to destruction of the faith, division of the nation, and loss of the people altogether. Accordingly the meaning of Torah was passed to the scholars of Israel, and it was commanded that the minority of them always submit to the majority.

The rest of your words: what you wrote about this; your charges against the innovations and changes in ancient Jewish customs that have regrettably begun to spread in most major cities where Jews live; your bitterness over indecisive rabbis; and your views on the simultaneous possibility of loving our kings, noblemen, and native land, and of hoping and believing in a return to Zion and Jerusalem by gathering the exiles from the four corners of the world—almost all that you say can be found in the writings of our great rabbi, the holy light of Israel, our master [Moses Sofer], the author of the *Chosom Sofer* (may the memory of the righteous and holy be for a blessing). . . .

This collection of writings from brilliant scholars and holy *gaonim*—men known not only for their sanctity and piety but also for their enormous generosity—should suffice to show the foolishness of those weak-willed [innovating] men against whom you poured out all your wrath at the end of your letter. But had you asked my advice, I would have told you not to argue with colleagues. Our rabbis told us [Brachot 63b] "Tell our brethren in the diaspora [if they listen to you, well and good; if not . . . let them all become renegades and say that they have no portion in the God of Israel."] You did your duty in your great efforts of a year ago; why challenge them any more? You, after all, are not their teacher, and they don't live in your area. Responsibility for them does not rest with you.

And now I come to the conclusion. Please don't be angry with me, my friend, if I forbear writing to you for two or three months. My work these days is great, and many besides yourself come to my office expecting me to answer them. I am unable to turn anyone away empty-handed.

This is migration season here: people move from house to house, court to court, and street to street. Should I too relocate my house and business, and you not know my address, please be so kind as to write, if you want something from me, to my honorable father and teacher, a man of righteousness, eminent in Torah and wondrous in deed, pious and modest, whose revered name is his glory, our master, Rabbi Isachar Baerish Weinberger, may his light shine forth, in the city of Zboró in the region of Sáros; or to my father-in-law, a rich and honorable man, Herrn Herrman Degen, Kniesen, Zips. They will always be able to tell you as much as you ask about me.

I close with the blessing of *shalom* [peace] to you and yours, as well as to all my loved ones and acquaintances there in your city of God. Your loyal, devoted, and loving friend,

MOSES WEINBERGER

Author's Notes

In the original text, these notes
appeared as footnotes.

    A. Perhaps they learned this inference from Deborah. Not Deborah the wife of Lapidot [Judges 4–5]—though like modern-day authors, she sang out in loud, clear Hebrew about dedicated public servants who came to help the Lord against the mighty, served as commanders and decision-makers, sat on saddle rugs ruling over clans, and stirred up all Israel. Being the rich owner of vineyards, dates, and olive trees, however, she sat aloft in Ataroth and knew nothing of authors' torments. They, rather, learned this via inference from a natural Deborah—a bee ["Deborah" in Hebrew means "bee"]. If a bee that extracts the purest honey in which no man can find fault is unhappy and storm-tossed, driven away like chaff, all for the sake of man—how much more entitled are men to try and brush off writers and intellectuals who sting like scorpions, hiss like serpents, and whose every word is a burning coal?

    B. One advertisement regularly seen in these journals reads in bold letters THE ORIENTAL THEATER. In the past most of our Jewish brethren didn't understand what this name meant. They suggested various theories; some even thought that it really referred to some means of solving the Oriental problem. Now, however, everybody knows that the reference relates to a Yiddish theater. The ad, with an image at the end, serves as a sort of advance man—"a flute before the altar [Mishnah Arachin 2:3]"—for which the performers pay good money. Still, the editors have acted dishonorably in this whole affair. Instead of placing this ad in a special section they let it wander from place to place, ending up each time in a different corner—sometimes among the sermons, the columns on ethics, and the words of Torah! This is intolerable. True, the ad's placement does not determine its worth—that, as readers will observe, wouldn't change no matter where the ad was. The message is always fresh, magnificent, sweet as a rose—in glory and praise of the actors themselves.
    A writer in one of the periodicals pours forth all his wrath against this theater, contending that every person who concerns himself even slightly with

taste should tear his clothes in mourning at its very existence. He shows clearly that of all those killed on stage, none received proper judgment according to law. Each death, rather, came about through armed robbery. None ever died a martyr's death. Each, rather, committed suicide over love or unappeased desire. Shall publishers therefore toss them roses or lay wreaths at their feet? Better neither to judge them nor blame them: just don't go where you don't belong. A Jewish periodical that regularly concerns itself with matters of holiness need not pretend to understand matters long considered by Jews to be frivolous. So what if actors' claims are false? What difference does it make? Does it make any difference to the editor or readers if Deborah died suddenly, was martyred, died because that's what the script called for, or if she is really alive but appears to be dead to make the play tragic? The publisher will earn his salary regardless.

Do we lose nothing by tampering with the facts? Do they lose nothing—our modest, righteous, and Orthodox brothers and sisters, our *chazanim, shochatim,* and half our rabbis—all of whom visit the theater occasionally, on Sabbath and holiday eves, on weekdays, before Monday and Thursday fasts of the pious, and on communal fast days, spending a great deal of money to bring themselves, their children and grandchildren? They want to train them, beginning in their youth, to recognize true beauty. Besides, they enjoy themselves a thousand times more there than they would from listening to a *magid*'s sermons, or from reading a high-minded periodical, or even from hearing a great and famous *chazan.* And it occurs not even to one person to ask the agonizing question, "Why couldn't Esther or Deborah die naturally?" Why couldn't they roll over in bed and fall dead of disease? Or another burning question, this one regarding the honest old man who committed suicide because he lacked the means to maintain himself: Was his brother a rich man who could honorably have supported him?

What do you want: Deborah to die, the diseased to find eternal rest from their pain, and the old man to win support from charity? Are you a stupid fool? Do you want to turn the theater into a hospital, an orphanage, or the [United] Hebrew Charities? Before you know it, you would have people escaping the theater as if a plague had hit it. The place would close down; there would be no more money for advertisements, rent, or salaries. Besides, what kind of enjoyment is there in a play about the sick, the orphaned, and the wretchedly poor? What pleasure is there in hearing the groans of the needy, or the sighing and howling of the miserable and helpless? And if our wealthy uptown brothers enjoy this, and squander thousands on it, why should it bother us? Have you not already told us not to follow in their paths? In short, the writer can get as angry as he pleases but as far as we are concerned, now as ever, all is lovely, pleasant, and sweet as honey. The publishers are innocent: they know their readers and their people. What is, is right; the world cannot be changed. Fools who come to wreak havoc will suffer the consequences in the end.

C.   We have elsewhere expanded on this point and shown from various authors and sources that the rabbis considered charity that does not lead to any good and laudable end to be mere squandering. They placed it at the opposite extreme from sustenance, the form of charity that God desires. The author of the *Sefer Hamidos [The Book of Ethical Qualities,* also known as *The Ways of the Righteous* (New York, 1969), p. 308] says that the squanderer is one who befriends the poor actively but not intelligently. What he means is that he does not make his contributions sensibly. A generous man does no good unless he is secretive about his gifts, giving only to the upright and honest; not to the hypocritical and wicked.

The *gaon* [Aryeh Leib Gunzberg], author of the *Ture Even*, says that generosity is an excellent attribute in man, requiring him to look at his fellows with a compassionate eye in order to find those basic needs that he lacks. This can be accomplished through deed, speech, and thought. Deed involves giving charity with one's own hand in the form of money, and physically helping those who need assistance. Speech involves speaking softly, pleasantly, and comfortingly, even if one cannot afford to provide basic needs. Thought involves thinking out a way through some pleasant means of achieving an end equally glorious and praiseworthy both to donor and to recipient. For every good deed that is accomplished without proper intelligence is unwanted by God; He has no desire to accept it.

The *Keli Yakar* [the commentary of Rabbi Solomon Luntschitz] at the end of [the biblical portion] *Mishpatim* [Exodus 23:5] wrote, based on a rabbinic homily, that one is required to help out only an ox prostrate under burden, not one that sat down of its own accord. From this one learns that a poor man who stands idle and does not support himself through his own labors, whatever work he is strong enough to perform, need not be given aid. (See also for enjoyment's sake Maimonides *Commentary on the Ethics of the Fathers*, [presumably 4:5].)

In our article, . . . which appeared last year, we wrote as follows: "Many here believe that all influence, righteousness, and charity flows from among our enlightened brethren. Their lips utter the words 'compassion,' 'mercy,' 'righteousness,' and 'pity' only to adorn the heads of innovators and reformers. They look upon Orthodox Jews here with scorn and contempt, as if to say that the Orthodox take no part in works of goodness and charity. But in fact such is not the case," as we expounded in detail. We concluded with the words "now as always the excellent attributes for which Jews have continually been praised remain in force. But we still complain about the great split that divides them, leading to their charity being spread to the winds. Theirs are not continuing ongoing activities, nor do we find among all the goodness and charity that they perform a single freestanding concrete project that can be seen, boasted about, and called their own. Were this not the case, if God would send an angel of salvation to bind all the disparate factions into a single unit to cooperate for a single purpose, then the money now dispersed could, without in any way being added to, favor all those dear ones who have now no part in it. Thousands of sick, unfortunate, and poor wretched folk could be aided."

D. "Rabbi Chama bar Chanina and Rabbi Hoshea were walking among the synagogues of Lod. Rabbi Chama bar Chanina said to Rabbi Hoshea, 'What a lot of money my ancestors spent here!' He replied, 'What a lot of lives your ancestors spent here! Were there not people [who needed the money] for studying Torah?' " [Talmud Yerushalmi, Pe'ah 8:8, Shekalim 5:4].

" 'Israel has ignored its Maker and built temples' [Hosea 8:14]—rather than giving [the money] to [poor] scholars for studying Torah" [Ibid. Shekalim 5:4, slightly variant text].

Editor's Notes

1. This question mark is in the original. It likely was added by someone who realized that no explicit discussion of *bodkim* can be found in the text.
2. Isidor Rosenthal was the son of Rev. Pesach Rosenthal (d. 1862), founder of the Talmud Torah.
3. I have been unable to identify Dov Kleif.
4. This estimate is too large. *Encyclopedia Judaica* (vol. 12, p. 1078) estimates the Jewish population of New York (including Brooklyn) at 80,000 in 1880 and 225,000 in 1890. Further on, Weinberger estimates the Jewish population (exclusive of Brooklyn) at 100,000 people, which is closer to the truth.
5. See editor's introduction, n. 7.
6. See editor's introduction, n. 35.
7. Jacob P. Solomon (1838–1909) was an immigrant from England, a noted lawyer, and founding editor of the *Hebrew Standard*. See *American Jewish Year Book* 6 (1904–5); 190; and J. D. Eisenstein, *Autobiography and Memoirs* (New York, 1929), p. 117 (in Hebrew).
8. Leo Merzbacher (1810–56) arrived in New York in the early 1840s and served congregations Rodeph Shalom and Anshe Chesed before being elected minister of the newly established Congregation Emanu-El. See Leon A. Jick, *The Americanization of the Synagogue* (Hanover, N.H., 1976), pp. 74–77.
9. "Ethical Culture" refers to the universalistic, socioreligious movement by that name, founded in 1876 by Felix Adler (1851–1933). See Benny Kraut, *From Reform Judaism to Ethical Culture: The Religious Evolution of Felix Adler* (Cincinnati, 1979).
10. Kasriel Sarasohn (1835–1905) was a leading Orthodox layman and a pioneering Yiddish journalist. See Victor Greene, "Becoming American," in *The Ethnic Frontier*, ed. Melvin G. Holli and Peter d'A. Jones (Grand Rapids, Mich., 1977), pp. 144–75.
11. Morris Wechsler (1849–1919) was born in Hungary and arrived in

America in 1885. He served as rabbi, printer, and newspaper editor, and helped to organize the Vaad Harabbonim Mahzike Hadath, the Orthodox Rabbinical Council of New York City, in 1896. Later he became involved in a *kashrus* scandal and was disgraced. *Jews and Judaism in New York* was printed by Wechsler's press. See Eisenstein, *Autobiography and Memoirs*, p. 55, and Harold P. Gastwirt, *Fraud, Corruption and Holiness* (New York, 1974), pp. 82–85.

12.   In the original text, the preceding paragraph was a footnote.

13.   Moses Mintz (1859–1930) and A. Braslavsky [Braslowsky] were active both in early Yiddish journalism and in the Jewish labor movement. See Melech Epstein, *Jewish Labor in U.S.A.* (New York, 1969); and Peter Wiernik, *History of the Jews in America* (New York, 1972), p. 396.

14.   On bookstores, see Eisenstein, *Autobiography and Memoirs,* p. 66; and Alexander Harkavy, "Chapters from My Life," *American Jewish Archives* 33 (April 1981), pp. 50–51.

15.   In the original text, the preceding anecdote was contained in a footnote.

16.   In the original text, the preceding anecdote was contained in a footnote.

17.   In the original text, the preceding digression was contained in a footnote.

18.   In the original text, the preceding anecdote was contained in a footnote.

19.   See Joseph Hirsh and Beka Doherty, *The First Hundred Years of the Mount Sinai Hospital of New York, 1852–1952* (New York, 1952).

20.   The preceding two paragraphs were originally contained in a footnote. The list of organizations was printed by Weinberger in English, and is reproduced in slightly revised form.

21.   Cf. J. H. Connelly, *Charities of the Hebrews of New York* (New York, 1888).

22.   See Zosa Szajkowksi, "The Attitude of American Jews to East European Jewish Immigration (1881–1893)," *Publications of the American Jewish Historical Society* 40 (March 1951): 226–27.

23.   In the original text, the preceding anecdote was contained in a footnote.

24.   This is the only chapter division in the original. For further discussion of this, see the editor's foreword to this volume; on *chazanim*, see the editor's introduction, n. 18.

25.   In the original, the preceding anecdote and aside were contained in a footnote.

26.   In the original, the preceding aside was contained in a footnote.

27.   Abraham Karp suggests that this stands for United Hebrew Orthodox Association, but he found no reference to the existence of such a group. Possibly Weinberger refers to the United Hebrew Orthodox Congregations, whose Board of Delegates, in 1879, attempted to induce Rabbi Meir Malbim (1809–79) to accept the post of New York chief rabbi. See Abraham J. Karp, "New York Chooses a Chief Rabbi," *Publications of the American Jewish Historical Society* 44 (1954): 129–35; Eugene Markovitz, "Henry Pereira Mendes: Architect of the

Union of Orthodox Jewish Congregations of America," *American Jewish Historical Quarterly* 55 (March 1966): 371–75; Eisenstein, *Autobiography and Memoirs*, pp. 252–53.

28.   In the original, the preceding aside was contained in a footnote.

29.   In the original, the words now in parentheses were contained in a footnote.

30.   Weinberger's eulogy of Perles appears in his *Dorosh Dorash Moshe* (New York, 1914), pp. 30–39.

Glossary

av bes din   chief judge

baal tefilah (baale tefilah)   reader(s) who lead the congregation in prayer

bar mitsvah (bnei mitsvah)   religious initiation ceremony(ies) for 13-year-old Jewish male(s)

batlan (im)   idler(s)

bes din   Jewish court

bes hamidrash (batei midrash)   house(s) of study

bimah   synagogue platform

chazan (im)   cantor(s)

cheder (chadarim)   religious elementary school(s)

dayan(im)   judge(s)

esrog(im)   citron(s)

gaon(im)   genius(es)

Gemara   second part of the Talmud; an amplification of the Mishnah

kashrus   the system of Jewish dietary laws (governing kosher food)

kehilah (kehilos)   Jewish community (communities)

kesubah   marriage document

kolel   advanced talmudic academy

lulav(im)   palm branch(es) used on Sukos

maftir   a section from prophetic writings recited on Sabbath and festival days

magid(im)   preacher(s)

matsah (matsos)   unleavened bread

megilah (megilos)   scroll(s); often refers to the Book of Esther *mezuzah (mezuzos)*   a case affixed to the doorpost containing the words of Deuteronomy 6:4–9; 11:13–21 written on a parchment scroll

mikvah (mikva'os)   ritual bath(s)

minyan(im)   prayer quorum(s), of ten males over the age of thirteen

Mishnah   collection of oral laws forming the first part of the Talmud

mitsvah (mitsvos)   commandment(s)

mohel (mohalim)   ritual circumciser(s)

musar   ethics, moral discipline

parnas(im)   synagogue president(s)

poskim   law codes, rabbinic codifiers

Rashi   Rabbi Shlomo Yitschaki, a great medieval commentator (1040–1105)

shamash(im)   sexton(s)

shechitah   ritual slaughtering

sh'ma   traditional Jewish confession of faith (Deuteronomy 6:4–9)

shmoneh esreh   eighteen benedictions, a central prayer in the Jewish liturgy

shochet (shochatim)   ritual slaughterer(s)

Shulchan Aruch   Joseph Karo's *Code of Jewish Law*

sidur (im)   prayerbook(s)

sukah (sukos)   tabernacle(s)

Sukos   Festival of Tabernacles

talis (taliyos)   prayer shawl(s)

tarfus   opposite of *kashrus*

Tosafos   a commentary on the Talmud

tsedakah   charity

tsitsis   ritual fringes

For more detailed explanations, see Philip Birnbaum, *A Book of Jewish Concepts* (New York, 1975).

Index